GRAIN OF EMPTINESS

MARTIN BRAUEN | MARY JANE JACOB

AIN OF EMPTINESS

ISM-INSPIRED CONTEMPORARY ART

RUBIN MUSEUM OF ART

This book is published in conjunction with an exhibition organized and presented by the Rubin Museum of Art, November 5, 2010, through April 11, 2011, curated by Martin Brauen.

ISBN-13: 978-0-9772131-9-1
ISBN-10: 0-9772131-9-6

Project Director: Helen Abbott
Project Assistants: Jonathan Kuhr and Lauren Smyth
Edited by: Neil Liebman
Designed by: Binocular, New York
Printed and bound in Italy

Library of Congress Cataloging-in-Publication Data
Jacob, Mary Jane.
Grain of emptiness : Buddhism-Inspired contemporary art / Mary Jane Jacob.
p. cm.
Published in conjunction with an exhibition held at the Rubin Museum of Art, Nov. 5, 2010–Apr. 11, 2011.
Includes bibliographical references.
ISBN-13: 978-0-9772131-9-1 (alk. paper)
ISBN-10: 0-9772131-9-6
1. Art, Modern—Buddhist influences—Exhibitions. 2. Art, Modern—21st century—Exhibitions. I. Rubin Museum of Art (New York, N.Y.) II. Title. III. Title: Buddhism-Inspired contemporary art.
N6497.J33 2010
709.05'10747471—dc22

2010033368

CONTENTS

FOREWORD

Donald Rubin

Shelley and my collection of Himalayan art began with a completely visceral response to a Tibetan *thangka* we saw in a gallery window, simply by chance. I'm not sure what exactly in me was responding to the painting, but whatever it was took me by storm, and I have been collecting art from the region ever since that afternoon in 1975. My point is that it was purely the aesthetics and not the religious message of Himalayan art that drew me to the form, at least on a conscious level.

Our exhibitions of traditional Himalayan art at the Rubin Museum of Art, while displaying many devotional works, do not usually focus on philosophical or religious themes. They are more about aesthetics, history, and culture than about religion.

And so it is interesting to me to see our first exhibitions of contemporary art and how they compare and contrast with our traditional presentations. The first one, *Tradition Transformed: Tibetan Artists Respond*, dealt head on with the issue of Buddhism and the codification of art making in relation to it. Most of the artists in the exhibition reinterpreted the idioms and messages of traditional Tibetan Buddhist art to create something new yet still Tibetan.

Now, in this second exhibition, curated by Martin Brauen, we present four Western artists and one Korean artist, who lives in New York and Seoul, whose work has been strongly influenced by Buddhism. Unlike the group of Tibetan artists who have transformed Buddhist tradition, these five artists have themselves been transformed by it, and this philosophical transformation can be seen in their work in *Grain of Emptiness: Buddhism-Inspired Contemporary Art.*

SUPPORTERS AND LENDERS

SUPPORTERS

Clinton Hill/Allen Tran Foundation
W.L.S. Spencer Foundation

LENDERS

Sanford Biggers
Theaster Gates
Kavi Gupta Gallery Chicago/Berlin
Atta Kim
Wolfgang Laib
Michael Rosenfeld Gallery, LLC
Sean Kelly Gallery, New York
Smithsonian American Art Museum
Solomon R. Guggenheim Museum
Tibet House, U.S. Collection
Whitney Museum of American Art

ACKNOWLEDGMENTS

Martin Brauen

I would like to thank all those who took part in this book project with so much commitment and engagement. This would include the artists Sanford Biggers, Theaster Gates, Atta Kim, Wolfgang Laib, the Kavi Gupta Gallery of Chicago/Berlin, the Sean Kelly Gallery, New York, and the Michael Rosenfeld Gallery, New York. I am also very appreciative of the following museums that graciously lent works of art by Charmion von Wiegand: the Smithsonian American Art Museum, the Solomon R. Guggenheim Museum, and the Whitney Museum of American Art. A special thank you must go to the Clinton Hill/Allen Tran Foundation and the W.L.S. Spencer Foundation, whose generous donations enhanced the contents of this catalog.

The following staff and contributors made this publication possible: Mary Jane Jacob, whose essays shed light on the nuances of the largely uninvestigated connections between Buddhism and the contemporary artists represented here; her able assistant, Rebecca Schlossberg; Kavie Barnes, who coordinated the exhibition and performed essential initial research of the artists and their influences, based on her knowledge of the field; Martin Willson who not only translated my essay very meticulously into English but who also made valuable suggestions to improve it; Helen Abbott and Neil Liebman, whose attention to the text gave it accessibility beyond an academic audience; Jonathan Kuhr and Lauren Smyth, who worked with the artists and editors to bring together vital image and graphic material; Joseph Cho and Stefanie Lew of Binocular for their elegant design achievements with the catalog.

To all these people and institutions I express my deepest gratitude. Emptiness became form thanks to their creativity and hard work.

PREFACE

Martin Brauen

FORM IS EMPTINESS, EMPTINESS IS FORM

Tibetan art is a means to an end. It is an aid that is supposed to make it possible for a meditating person to realize the buddhahood inherent in each of us, and with that to achieve the realization of the emptiness (*shunyata*) of all existence. Yet Tibetan art stands out for an incredible variety of forms and colors. Is this a contradiction? No, for this fullness of form, as manifested for example in a mandala, is emptiness, and emptiness is this fullness of form. It says in the *Heart Sutra* (*Prajnaparamita Hridaya Sutra*):

> Form is emptiness and the very emptiness is form;
> emptiness does not differ from form, form does not differ from emptiness;
> whatever is form, that is emptiness, whatever is emptiness, that is form.[1]

Thus it is possible for a museum devoted to Tibetan art to open its doors to artists who simplify or abstract form so much that no perfect Buddha image, no bodhisattva, no Tara, or no wrathful deity is recognizable in their work. Instead, the visitor encounters paintings consisting of simple shapes—triangles, circles, squares (Charmion von Wiegand); objects of natural materials such as a square slab of marble, whose slightly hollowed upper surface is filled each day with fresh milk (Wolfgang Laib); photographs that hint at another reality behind the reality they ostensibly depict (Atta Kim); a lotus flower etched on glass, which refers as much to the painful and terrible past of African Americans, that is to say, to slavery, as it does to Buddhism (Sanford Biggers); and a video installation that follows one African American Buddhist and four African American Christians through their meditative rituals, which are solemn and private, into a space where their voices become an exploration of culturally specific music practices, interacting with other musicians and singers (Theaster Gates).

Wolfgang Laib, one of the artists represented here, told me in conversation that his *Milkstone* (FIG. 1)—so he thought—represented fundamental Buddhist ideas better than a Buddha statue (FIG. 2).[2] At first I could not understand what he meant. But on longer reflection I discerned the meaning of his words, especially when I cast my mind's eye over the development of the Buddha image in the course of time. In India, for a long time the bodily depiction of the Buddha was frowned upon. It was not the person of the Buddha that was the focus of interest, but his ideas, which—according to the views of that time—could not be portrayed pictorially. If the Buddha were represented, it would be only in symbolic form, not least because the Buddha himself disapproved of representations of himself. After his death, one simply depicted his footprints, the Bodhi tree beneath which he had attained enlightenment, an empty seat under the Bodhi tree, a lotus bud, or the Wheel of the Teaching, which recalls the Buddha's first sermon. The bodily form of the Buddha was taboo. This is also confirmed by the following conversation between the Buddha and his disciple Subhuti:

> "What do you think, Subhuti, can the Tathagata be seen by his perfect set of marks [i.e., the thirty-two bodily marks of a great being]?"
>
> Subhuti replied: "No, Lord, he cannot. Why is that? What has been taught by the Tathagata as the perfect set of marks, that is truly a non-set-of-marks."
>
> The Lord said to Venerable Subhuti: "Wherever there is a perfect set of marks, Subhuti, there is falsehood, wherever there is non-set-of-marks there is no falsehood. Hence the Tathagata is to be seen from non-marks as marks."[3]

And in the same text, the Buddha confirms what was said before:

> Those who saw me by my form
> And those who followed me by voice
> Were engaged in wrong practices.
> Those people will not see me.[4]

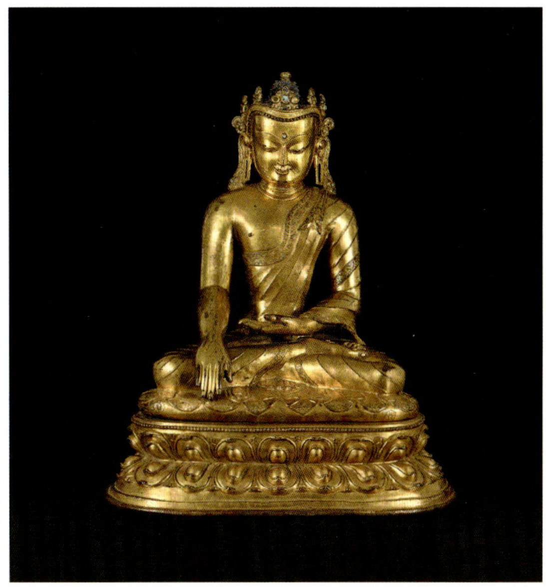

FIGURE 1
Wolfgang Laib. *Milkstone,* 2010. White marble, milk. 2⅜ × 20½ × 24½ in. (6 × 52 × 62 cm).
© Wolfgang Laib. Courtesy of the artist and Sean Kelly Gallery, New York

FIGURE 2
Buddha Shakyamuni. Tibet; 14th century. Gilt copper alloy. 20 × 17 × 12 in. (50.8 × 43.2 × 30.5 cm).
Rubin Museum of Art. C2001.10.2 (HAR 65025)

Not until the first century before Christ, in Gandhara and Mathura in northern India, did people begin to depict the bodily manifestation of the Buddha in a realistic yet idealized form. From then on, Buddha statues were embodiments of the ethics and doctrine taught by the Buddha.

From time immemorial, therefore, both word *and* image have been bearers or mediators of Buddhist ideas or ideals. As we have seen, the image was at first aniconic, then iconic, but later on, in certain Buddhist schools such as Zen Buddhism, it sometimes took on aniconic characteristics once again. It is different in Tibetan Buddhism. Tibetan religious art is remarkable for a distinctive realism, a kind of *symbolic* realism, as it seeks to portray a reality different from the "normal" one and displays a rich language of symbols. But for all its realistic depictions, this art, too, is basically a mirror that reflects the reality of all phenomena: Emptiness.

GRAIN

The title of the exhibition, *Grain of Emptiness*, takes up this central Buddhist concept of emptiness but enlarges on it with the word "grain." This word has a double meaning. When one hears the word "grain" one thinks first of all of a grain of cereal, a grain of barley for example. Understood in this way, a grain is something that is really small, a mere dot, but has the potential for something much bigger. In the tiny space of a grain of cereal slumbers the entire plant—and even more: innumerable further plants that can arise from the first one. In each and every thing, even the smallest and the highly ephemeral, all things are contained. For Wolfgang Laib, who uses pollen grains in his art, pollen is "the most fragile, the most temporary, but the essence of life of the plants, like the milk for animals and human beings."[5]

The title of the exhibition indicates this figuratively: every thing, even the smallest, contains from a Buddhist point of view buddhahood, or suchness (*tathata*),[6] or emptiness, a concept that we shall go into in more detail below.

A second meaning of "grain" is in connection with the structure or texture of certain materials: for example, the grain of cloth, of woven fabric, is the warp and weft threads making up the cloth. This image too makes sense in the present case: a fabric is a weave of threads, which only in their totality amount to a useful whole. Each thread is important for the integrity of the fabric, each thread is dependent on the immediately adjacent threads, which in turn are for their part dependent on other threads. One could also say that the threads are interdependent. This recalls the old Buddhist law of *pratityasamutpada*, the law of interdependence or of dependent arising. Everything is brought about through a number of conditioning factors, everything is dependent on and relates to something else.[7]

As Nagarjuna demonstrated, the law of interdependence and the concept of emptiness are two sides of the same coin. *Grain* (warp and weft) *of Emptiness* as a metaphor for the law of interdependence and *Grain* (seed) *of Emptiness* as emptiness, all-pervading and contained in the smallest atom, are two complementary, noncontradictory concepts. The title *Grain of Emptiness*, which initially seems to be a conundrum, or *koan*, becomes understandable.

A photograph by Atta Kim may clarify the same teaching further. Atta Kim photographed an important and lengthy Buddhist text, the *Avatamsaka Sutra,*[8] page after page, and superimposed the individual images in a single photograph[9] in which two blocks lying side by side can be made out, each displaying ten vertical, grayish, fuzzy lines (FIG. 3). The text, which expounds in detail in 5,844 pages how, as Buddha taught, all living beings carry within themselves Buddha nature and all phenomena are mutually originating and interdependent, has become an abstract texture. Each of the vertical gray lines is the sum of 5,844 superimposed pages of text written in Chinese characters. Every page photographed and every line in it testifies to the wisdom of the Buddha. But what are these sentences, these words and characters, in fact, in reality? They also, Atta Kim seems to be saying with his photomontage, are empty. When writing in English, we assemble characters that we call letters into words, we assign meaningful content to accumulations of words—sentences—and by joining sentences together we fashion theories. But basically the theories, sentences, words, and letters are empty, as anything composite is relative and transitory.

What this text expresses in many words on innumerable pages is contained in this one photograph—reduced to the basic statement: everything is mutually dependent. All the individual words and pages together give the book its meaning. And—according to Buddhism—whatever is dependent upon something else cannot be truly existent—it is empty.[10]

Atta Kim appears to be expressing something similar with his series in which he photographed busy parts of cities, not taking snapshots but exposing the film for eight hours (see PLATES 14, 15).[11] Motionless things such as the houses are clearly visible, while everything that moves appears to form a gray-brown haze. Cars, motorcycles, bicycles, people, and animals that were within the view of the camera during the eight hours of exposure form an amorphous mass. They appear to be nonexistent, leaving a barely visible trace of transience. If one thinks out Atta Kim's experiment further and imagines a camera stationed in the same place for far longer—50, 100, 1,000, 10,000 years—then even the supposedly static, motionless, and everlasting would no longer be visible. For even these things change: buildings are extended, demolished, and replaced, or a town is completely abandoned and falls into ruin. Form becomes emptiness. Form is emptiness.

The feeling of connectedness also characterizes the creations of Sanford Biggers and Theaster Gates—even if the connection with the concept of dependent arising (*pratityasamutpada*) or emptiness (*shunyata*) is less obvious in their case. The fleetingness of their art is revealed in their preference to create art about time, performance art, which appears to demonstrate not so much the emptiness of the material as the relativity and thus the emptiness of time. One could perhaps say, to use a Buddhist term, that they show the suchness (*tathata*)[12] of time.

EMPTINESS

I have already used the term "emptiness" several times, without explaining it in the Buddhist context. This was deliberate, for emptiness is one of the most complex concepts in Buddhism, best approached in a roundabout fashion.

Tibetan Buddhists regard what is generally called reality as being without essence, without a stable core or—to use a Buddhist expression—as empty or void. Out of the wrong interpretation of perceptions and human longings arise contradictions, which the Buddhist seeks to recognize

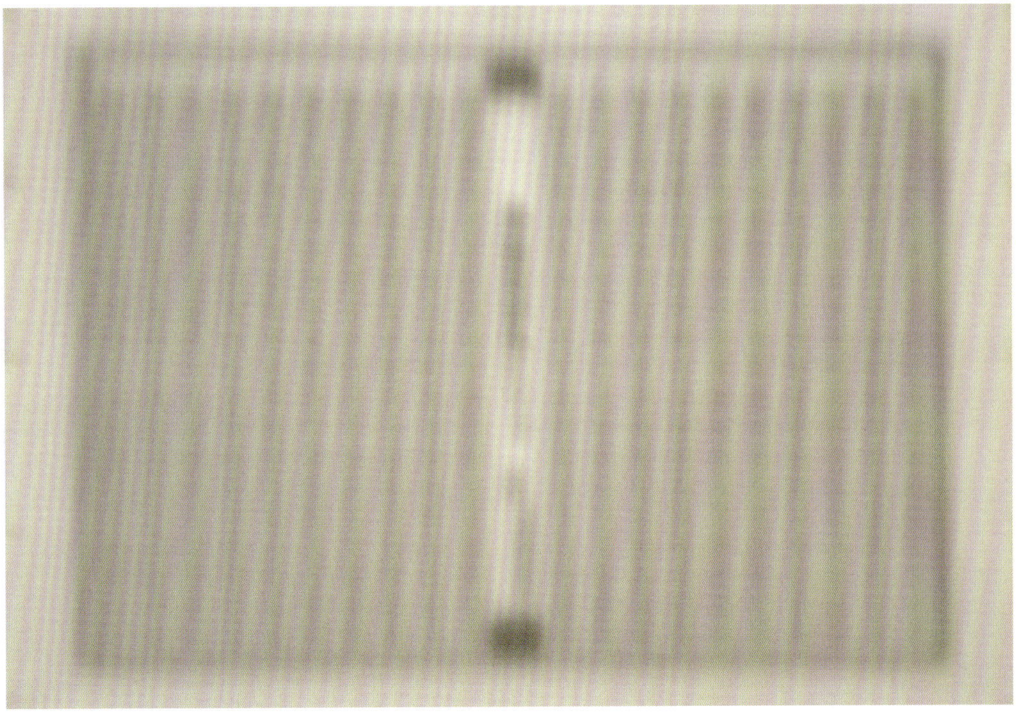

FIGURE 3
Atta Kim. *ON-AIR Project 5844, The Avatamsaka Sutra,* 2007.
Chromogenic print. 35⅜ × 51½ in. (89.9 × 130.8 cm). Courtesy of the artist

with the aid of meditation and an in-depth, systematic analysis of the phenomena. By meditating and analyzing, the meditator grasps that behind what we call real exists instead emptiness, or the void (*shunyata*).

But how can emptiness be reality? From among the various concepts of emptiness, we will draw on the widely held concept of the Prasangika-madhyamika School, of which Nagarjuna is regarded as the most prominent advocate. This school regards phenomena and beings as empty, insofar as they have no inherent or objective existence of their own. It is not a matter of the complete nonexistence of a phenomenon but of the lack of a self. The Prasangika concept does not put into question the world of things and people around us but rather the way we see the world.

Although, or just because, emptiness is such a central idea in Buddhism, approaching this Buddhist principle is hard for several reasons: first, because emptiness evades definition, it resists description or analysis. Emptiness is beyond conceptuality, it is nonconceptuality *par excellence*. Second, in the West emptiness tends to be equated with nothingness, a way of interpretation that can scarcely stand up to more precise examination but is nevertheless widespread. And third, even within Buddhism emptiness is a concept that is discussed and described in a variety of ways, which makes clarification more difficult.

To make the idea of emptiness more comprehensible, I shall have recourse to a personal experience, which I shall relate to an example from the Tibetan reformer Tsongkhapa.

One morning, as I was waking up in a bedroom in Greece and looking up at the ceiling, I saw on a beam a small scorpion. I knew that there were scorpions in that area, I had heard about them, but I had never seen one. There I lay motionless on the bed, with above me—not two meters away—one of those tiny poisonous creatures that I really did not like. What if the scorpion suddenly fell down? How should I react? What should I do?

I waited and waited, hoping that the wretched creature might move and signal to me whether it wanted to have an argument with me. Nothing happened. Eventually I dared to get up from the bed, then slowly a doubt arose: was this thing that I had seen as a scorpion dead? Was it actually a scorpion? If it was not a scorpion, what then?

Look harder! I told myself.

Yes—it really was one of those poisonous little beasts. I could make out the slightly raised tail and the hint of a leg … but where were the other legs?

More waiting. Just a bit closer … look, observe, and wait.… Then at last, alarm over! What I had taken for a scorpion was in fact a wisp of cloth that had caught on the beam when it was being dusted.

After I had gotten over my scare, a Buddhist parable came into my mind. It is not, however, about a wisp of cloth turning into a scorpion but about ascribing the existence of a snake to a rope in the twilight. With this parable, the Tibetan reformer Tsongkhapa sought to demonstrate how self-existence is falsely ascribed to things. A rope is turned by my consciousness into a snake. Therefore, reality is not as I perceive it.

You might say, it is true that the scorpion I thought I saw was not a scorpion or that the snake I interpret as a rope is not an actual snake; but if I took other examples, then the claim that reality is not what I see and perceive would fall apart. For example, you could argue, the room that you are in while you are reading these lines exists. Likewise the chair you are sitting on and the lamp that lights the room. My error, you would continue, was that I saw an object incorrectly and consequently drew a false conclusion. I was taken in by an optical illusion, a phantom, a delusion.

With this we have fallen into the middle of a complex of questions that is of central importance in Buddhist philosophy: What is reality? What is truth? These questions were debated among the Buddhist scholars of Tibet with great vigor and much controversy—sometimes with arguments similar to those in Western philosophy.

But what has my scorpion experience got to do with it? The Tibetan reformer Tsongkhapa should clarify this for us. About the rope-snake parable he writes the following—though it fits my wisp-of-cloth-scorpion experience just as well:

> Take, for example, the case of an imaginary snake that is mistakenly perceived as a rope. If we … try to analyze what the snake itself is like in terms of its own nature, its features cannot be analyzed, inasmuch as a snake is simply not present in that object.

Now follows the essential sentence that goes beyond what has been said already:

> It is similar with regard to all phenomena.… [When] we analyze the objects in and of themselves, asking, "What is the manner of being of these phenomena?" We find that they are not established in any way. Yet ignorance does not view it in this way; it apprehends each phenomenon as having a manner of being such that it can be understood in and of itself, without being posited through the force of a conventional consciousness.[13]

Expressed another way, and applied to my scorpion experience: what we call a scorpion (and now I am not talking about a wisp of cloth any longer) has no true, final, or substantial self-existence, no unitary essence *or* no identity. It is put together out of innumerable individual parts and characteristics—such as, it is living, it is thin and elongated, it is slightly curved, it has eight legs, pincers, a kind of tail, etc. Only by the joining together of the individual parts and individual characteristics does there arise a, as it were, synthetic structure that one calls "scorpion." Only this joining together of the individual different parts means the perception of the phenomenon "scorpion." Only labeling by way of concepts, sub-concepts, and sub-sub-concepts allows the scorpion to, so to speak, come into being. The thing "scorpion" exists for us solely through the joining together of the various different features and characteristics.

There is no doubt about the relative existence of phenomena that are simultaneous and appear together. The head of the scorpion, which makes up one part of what I designate a scorpion, is in existence, but this head is in turn a joining together of eyes, mouth, etc. This means that the individual phenomena and sub-phenomena are not negated (at least in this school), so one cannot speak of nihilism.

What is analyzed and negated is our *interpretation* of phenomena and sub-phenomena and the attribution of concepts as if these appearances were independent, self-contained entities. Our consciousness, our thoughts, "creates" the scorpion and, in a very general sense, what we call reality. Or in other words, we recognize because we interpret; we recognize because we make classifications.

However, from the Buddhist point of view, it is held that:

> As stars, a fault of vision, as a lamp,
> A mock show, dew drops, or a bubble,
> A dream, a lightning flash, or cloud,
> So should one view what is conditioned.[14]

It is therefore a matter of recognizing the illusionary nature of phenomena, of discerning that everything is composite and because of that exists in dependence on something else. It is necessary to recognize how phenomena depend on thought, how they are given their existence only through our classifications and categorizations, how we attribute to phenomena their characteristics and with that their existence.

The methods that Buddhism offers for realizing absolute truth are meditation on emptiness and the analysis of phenomena, which leads to gaining special insight and to the understanding of the "signless" or emptiness. The second method is the way of reasoning, thinking, considering, of argument and counter-argument.

* * *

The artists living in the West who are being presented here also offer us possibilities of looking at phenomena or appearances in other than conventional ways, of looking behind phenomena so to speak. But they do so in a different way from Buddhist thinkers—not with words, but with their art. They challenge us in their art "to see reality in a different way," as Wolfgang Laib puts it, for whom "The Ephemeral is Eternal,"[15] just as in the spirit of Nagarjuna, for whom there is no difference between conventionalities and suchness.[16] The artists represented here lay bare the impermanence and interrelation of phenomena, like, for example, Atta Kim. And, like Theaster Gates, they show the blurring boundaries of concepts that at first glance look so different, disconnected and incoherent, as the gospel singers who incorporate Buddhist chanting. They point to how the painful, continuous flow of life, *samsara*, is most closely bound up with the highest state, *nirvana*, or the supreme realization of emptiness, like Sanford Biggers with his *Lotus*. This overwhelmingly positive Buddhist symbol for purity, perfection, and stainless wisdom that has realized the nature of emptiness is made up of drawings symbolizing the suffering of black slaves. With this work of art, the artist seems to be expressing what Nagarjuna has described as follows:

> There is no difference at all between *samsara* [the continuous flow of life, the circle of births] and *nirvana* … not even the most subtle difference is found between the two.[17]

Or, as phrased by Charmion von Wiegand, one of the artists represented here, who has been influenced by Tibetan Buddhism: "The artist does give the viewer a new way to see."

That is the very point of this exhibition.

Translated by Martin Willson

Notes to the Preface

1 *Heart Sutra*, 10–14, translated from the Sanskrit by Edward Conze (*Buddhist Wisdom Books*, George Allen & Unwin, 1958, repr. Harper Torchbooks, 1972). The text continues that what was said about form is also valid for the four other *skandhas* that together with form constitute a human being: feelings, perceptions, volitions, and consciousness.

2 This conversation took place in April 2010 at Wolfgang Laib's home.

3 The *Vajracchedika Prajnaparamita Sutra* (*The Diamond Sutra*), chapter 5. Martin Willson's translation from the Sanskrit. I referred to the translation and commentary by Edward Conze (*Buddhist Wisdom Books* and "Some More Comments on the Diamond Sutra" in *Vajra*, 3, July 1976, 3–12) and to the Tibetan translation. My paraphrase: As long as one sees his 32 bodily marks as truly existent, one does not see the Buddha (Tathagata). Only "non-marks," whose emptiness of truly existent marks one sees, can lead one to him. As Conze explains, this chapter points out "that it would be a mistake to place the Buddha among the false, conditioned things, and that this is done by concentrating on his visible, distinctive features. Our conception of the Buddha must do justice to him as the unconditioned Absolute." (MW)

4 *The Diamond Sutra*, chapter 26, translation details as note 3.

5 Letter to the author, December 17, 2009.

6 The word 'Suchness' or 'Thusness' (*tathata*) is an adequate term for the Ultimate, and thence for Emptiness. The term 'Suchness' is 'neutral', not evoking any image, as no features or characteristics can be attributed to it.

7 Interestingly, a similar conception of the world is held by modern physicists, like Heisenberg: "The world thus appears as a complicated tissue of events, in which connections of different kinds alternate or overlap or combine, and thereby determine the texture of the whole." (quoted by Trinh Xuan Than in: *The Quantum and the Lotus*, 2001, 72).

8 The oldest parts go back to the beginning of our common era. The final text composed of a number of originally independent scriptures of diverse provenance was combined probably in Central Asia in the late third or the fourth century CE.

9 *ON-AIR Project 5844*, 2007.

10 This is, of course, not the only statement in the *Avatamsaka Sutra*, but it is a very central one.

11 For this the aperture of the camera was minimized and Atta has put several gelatin filters on the lens to reduce the light intensity.

12 See note 6.

13 According to Guy Newland, *Appearance Reality, The Two Truths in the Four Buddhist Tenet Systems*, 1999, 78. For better understanding of the translation, the text has been slightly abridged and a few brackets that were present in the original translation have been deleted.

14 *Diamond Sutra* (*Vajracchedika Prajnaparamita Sutra*), chapter 32, conclusion, translated by Edward Conze (*Buddhist Wisdom Books*). See his commentary for explanations of the nine examples.

15 This was the title of an extensive retrospective of Wolfgang Laib's work at the Beyeler Foundation, Riehen, Switzerland (27.11.2005–26.2.2006), and of the book on his work that was published on that occasion, Hatje Cantz Verlag, 2005.

16 In Nagarjuna's *Essay on the Mind of Enlightenment*, which says: Suchness is not observed as different from conventionalities, because conventionalities are explained as emptiness, and just emptiness is conventionalities. See C. Lindtner's translation, according to Guy Newland, 1999, 87.

17 See David Snellgrove, *Indo-Tibetan Buddhism*, 1987/2002, 83.

INTRODUCTION

Mary Jane Jacob

The five artists in this exhibition share a great deal, including a desire to give a form to the concept of emptiness. They seek to show us something beyond the material world, "beyond the world of appearances" (Charmion von Wiegand). These artists know that in emptiness everything is possible. They are each driven by a need to understand themselves as part of a greater whole, of a "new unity" (von Wiegand); they desire to understand how the impermanence of life is not an end, but a way of seeing "the inner world of things" (Atta Kim), to know that they are a part of a continuum, and then "continue that continuum of energy or sensory exchange" (Sanford Biggers). Imagining things they had in some way "always believed in" (Theaster Gates) and seeking to represent it, even though it is of "a measure outside of time and outside of place" (Wolfgang Laib), they choose art as their means. Thus the very creation of art becomes a necessity for them. It is of personal necessity, too, that they share moments of awareness with others. So while they make art for their own understanding, their work is ultimately intended to communicate their insights with others, and in this, they reaffirm one of the essential reasons why we have art.

Buddhism is not a religious pursuit for these five artists: it has been a "guidepost" (Gates) and, mixed with other spiritual traditions and ways of life, echoes are felt across cultures as "connections and forces arise" (Laib) and a "visceral affinity" (Biggers) emerges. And when these echoes are perceived, the artists attune themselves and allow these associations to resonate deeply and slowly. Their paths, idiosyncratic but not unique, may be an outcome of a wider sublimation of the spiritual that modern society imposes. In our secular world the overt expression of spirituality is often deemed to be polarities of culture—either right-wing fundamentalism or a New-Age modality. But a need to understand one's place as part of a bigger scheme has *always* been with us. These artists chose a path of reflection, cultivating a self-reflecting mind (or what has been termed the self-conscious unconscious), determining their own path in a world that may be without an all-knowing God but which is not without spirituality. And they do so purposefully, valuing social intent and allowing it to be an inner compass for their artistic pursuits.

Committed to a way of working and of being, they have chosen art as a practice, a philosophy, and a way of life. In this, focus and clarity are critical. They cultivate attention, in part, by engaging with the practice of Buddhism—it brings them "equilibrium" and "sustenance," is "centering" and "grounding" (Biggers). Buddhism helps locate the unknowable, making it known as it is reflected in everyday ways, as we see the spiritual in our midst, manifest in "a kind of ordinariness that is seemingly more mundane" (Gates), like "simply looking at the milk" (Laib). Looking to where the spiritual resides on earth, they find that life itself holds many answers. But to perceive this, awareness is the key. Awareness comes from a practiced mind and awareness connotes openness: a mind open to what life brings at the moment "open to receive, and listen, and sense things that are around you" (Biggers), and an openness to what things experienced now can mean over time. These artists have come to know, too, that art—maybe more than anything else—has power because it is "a completely open path" (Laib).

At the beginning of the last century, the American philosopher John Dewey (who looked to Eastern philosophy, as well as to the West, in trying to create a philosophy for modern American life) also found art the necessary means for living life, and art is also necessary in philosophy's pursuit of understanding life. Dewey offered this thought to the field: "For philosophy like art moves in the medium of imaginative mind, and, since art is the most direct and complete manifestation there is of experience *as* experience, it provides a unique control for the imaginative ventures of philosophy."[1] Art can evoke the wholeness of life, what Dewey called continuity. For him, art "is the fusion of life and learning, doing and undergoing. Art expresses what life is and brings it to clarity and completion."[2] A life path through art allows for the cultivation of self and offers the ability to realize new potentialities in the process of our becoming. This process, being continuous, is always in need of renewing, and in this, "the new" serves as a stimulus—awakening us, transforming the present moment, intensifying it, making it meaningful, and at times even fulfilling our desire to understand more deeply. When this occurs, our experience is reoriented and we see anew, "in another way," with "new vision" that changes "accustomed points of reference" (von Wiegand), and gives us a "totally different perspective" (Laib).

To make the most of experience and have it be transformative in positive ways, we need to cultivate presence of mind. The presence of mind of these artists not only erupts in the conception of an idea for a work of art but also, importantly, is sustained throughout the act of making. The very act of doing cultivates the mind, and not "on some kind of theoretical level" (Gates), it is "not some philosophical structure" (Laib), but stimulates in tangible ways, for "art always has one foot on the ground" (von Wiegand). Thus, the process of making is the art as well as the final result, the experience of doing is part of the whole: means and end are one flowing together. Dewey said: "The process is art and its product, no matter at what stage it be taken, is a work of art,"[3] and we see this in their works. "The process itself is the experience; it's important to experience it, just as in the way we live our lives. To only see the end wouldn't be the life in which we want to live. We want to experience" (Kim). Moreover the process is art *and* is life. So there is the need on the part of these artists to get the most out of the doing, the fullest experience. This phenomenon is achieved when "your interior and your exterior meet," "you get in harmony" (von Wiegand), and you are "in the void" (Biggers). Then the mind-in-making, being fully present in the experience of the process, gives to the work of art its presence, too. It is this quality that draws us into a work that first was a revelation for the artist as it emerged from a process of creative inquiry. At that point the work of art "has its own energy" (Kim); "those are the real power objects" (Biggers).

Holding on to moments of insight and understanding gained through experience can be elusive. The mind loses focus, so we have to practice. While meditation is one way, looking at art is another powerful means—"using [art] as a mechanism to channel focus" (Biggers). When the work of art is the embodiment of the artist's insights, the effect is compounded. And this is the case with these artists. They know that while they pursue a personal path, their insights might equally be of significance to others, a journey that "can be as much inward facing as it is collaborative, sharing, and communal" (Gates).

Being a part of the times in which they live (and any time posing seemingly impassable problems), these artists also have some messages they wish to convey to the world, and they trust that art can speak to intangible but essential realms of life because of the energy they believe it can possess and which they strive to engender. They know that in certain ways (and perhaps in no uncertain terms) "art changes the world" (Laib). This is not a moralistic directive, although moral values are at stake; their art does not give answers but suggests ways of seeing and perhaps living. For as Dewey believed, too: "Only imaginative vision elicits the possibilities that are interwoven within the texture of the actual. The first stirrings of dissatisfaction and the first intimations of a better future are always found in works of art."[4]

At that juncture—in the communication of meanings we can take from art and into life—art museums can have a role to play. Museums are sites for experiences: experience in the present moment and in the presence of art. They can enable experience to unfold in open and new ways, because they can offer "concentration and calmness, an intensity that does not otherwise exist" (Laib) and allow clarity to emerge no matter whether the work is itself quietly contemplative or interactive and loud, that is, when the experience is devoted to art and unencumbered by the institutional noise of the museum experience (which is quite often not the case). Moreover, museums are not places of lived-with experience, so the separation they force between life and art is to the detriment of our experience.[5] Yet museums have something to provide as "intermediaries" (Biggers). In their remove, they can reframe life so that we can see it perhaps for the first time, or perhaps it just seems so, and we can make connections in new ways when we walk back out on the street. This focused, concentrated experience of viewing art—and museums can be a place for this—strengthen our perception and offer a changed consciousness about the world in which we must always reimmerse ourselves. That understanding, if only at moments, is what these five artists offer us, too.

WOLFGANG LAIB

Wolfgang Laib moves between spaces and realms: living quietly in the country and having major shows in cities; traveling regularly to India and other distant places, while residing in Germany; working with tangible, elemental materials that he gathers around him, yet evoking something other worldly. It seems his good fortune to have grown up from age ten in a Bauhaus-style glass house fused with nature, to have had a father who was a doctor and who made esoteric white paintings and sculpture, and to have had as a neighbor a painter who had studied Chinese philosophy, had a modest lifestyle, and just happened to have Kasimir Malevich paintings under the bed.[1] The dye was cast.

Laib traveled the mind, studying Eastern philosophy, Indian languages and culture, archaeology and art history, as well as medicine. But early on he also went with his family to far away places, to the Middle East and Asia. He returned years later to one of these locations that he had visited at age fifteen—Konya, Turkey, the spiritual site of the Sufi mystic poet Jalal-ud-din Rumi—to create there one of his first sculptures. Being in other places, in touch with the actual, is an essential experience for this artist to find inspiration, but it is even more essential to his being. Laib has been drawn to cultures that, to him, are filled with meaning and that transcend place and time to illuminate his own world. "I was interested in non-European cultures because I feel that if you take them really seriously they offer a big challenge to our own cultures. They can give a totally different perspective on what you think is right and wrong and what you know. I think this is what art brings to society. Something totally new," he has said.[2]

One way that Wolfgang Laib brings his art into relation with that of other cultures is through a shared use of pure geometry and saturated color, not as representations of something in the everyday world but to stand for something beyond what is otherwise formless. "For me, the simpler the work's statement the more levels it can have."[3] Over time, in culture upon culture, these forms have earned the designation of archetype; they have demonstrated potency and legibility across the ages. Moreover, of his use of stupas, ziggurats, pyramids, and staircases, he has said: "I extract them from the historical context and embed them in the present, in my life. In the process, connections and forces arise, quite new contexts that are independent of the here and now."[4] Their meanings already exist within human civilization, coming from a place of collective knowledge. So they are unifying. The artist has said: "It is great if the same or similar thoughts and ideas appear in quite different places and at quite different times—and it is even greater if you, as an individual, are part of a whole."[5]

Wolfgang Laib has gravitated to a simple life, too, or so it would seem. A life lived in touch with the earth, it is filled with a knowing awareness of and participation in life's forces of transformation, change, and continuity. Buddhism is not a religion he practices but aspects of it can be found in his life practice. Some have remarked on his monkish demeanor, the retreat-like aspect of his residence. Personally, he admires the figure of St. Francis, the monk who communed with nature and whose enlightenment was signified by the stigmata, visiting his sanctuary home in Assisi on several occasions. If removal from the world lends focus to our experience, then Laib's choice of a quiet rural location for his home and studio is a good one, as he said, "simply because of the intensity I can experience here, and that is very, very important."[6] His disciplined method of making art not only demands this silence but also requires being in harmony with the patterns of nature. If spiritual practice is a path to a more fulfilling life and wider understanding of things, then Laib's way of being—not just where he lives but how he is—reaches if not surpasses that definition.[7] "My life is my work," he has said,[8] a remark that recalls something the artist once said about the culture of India to which he is repeatedly drawn: "Art is life in itself."[9] And if, as John Dewey said, art is the experience of experience,[10] then Laib's experience is the art that he gives us. Yet what is this life, this way of being, that Laib has found from which his art springs and which he offers to us?

A personal, physical engagement in making the work is essential to Laib. He does not describe the process as art or identify it as performance. But his very act of making is, nonetheless, the conveyance by which he infuses his work with meaning. All his processes are slow; we might

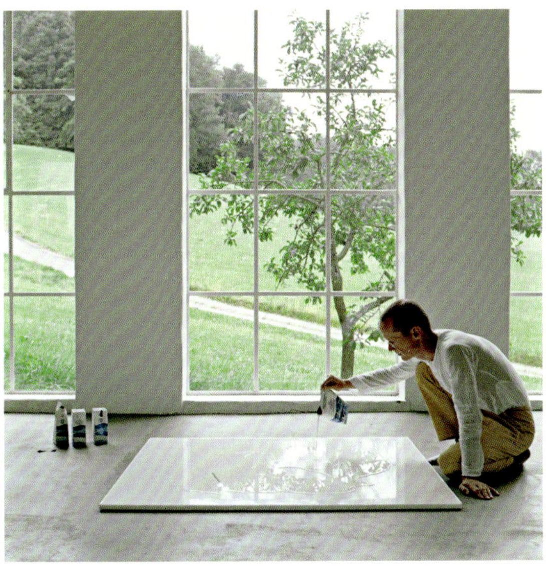

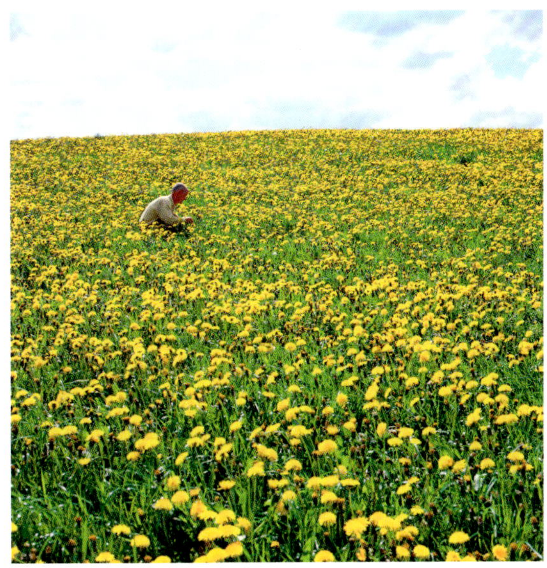

FIGURE 4
Wolfgang Laib. Laib pouring the milk for *Milkstone*, 1987–90. White marble, milk. Installation in the artist's studio. ¾ × 48 × 51⅛ in. (2 × 122 × 130 cm). © Wolfgang Laib. Courtesy of the artist and Sean Kelly Gallery, New York

FIGURE 5
Wolfgang Laib. Laib collecting pollen in the dandelion meadow. © Wolfgang Laib. Courtesy of the artist and Sean Kelly Gallery, New York

call them meditative methods or see these actions as akin to rituals. Laib's engagement with the process of making extends to the acquisition of materials, too, especially the unimaginable task of collecting the minute, fugitive grains of pollen. Through this task the artist actually becomes a part of the natural processes of time, processes that elude the rest of us out of habit or through technology. And Laib's art-making practice "enables a totally different idea of what a day is, or what your life is about, or what work could be or what you would like to achieve."[11]

For his medium, Laib has looked to the use of staples of life in Indian devotional practices that nourish the soul as well as the body. Milk, pollen, rice, which he frequently chooses, are real and of the world. Each is a living substance and, life giving, possesses an energy that spawns offspring of infinite lineage and magnitude. In his "Milkstones," begun in 1975, milk is received by a rectangular receptacle, its delicate marble casing mimicking the translucence of the milk (FIG. 4). They unite: "The milk is there for some hours and becomes one with the stone."[12] This stasis of this life is not for long. Exposed, it needs frequent tending so as not to turn from sweet to sour. Its impermanent state underscores the fleetingness of the lives of the beings it otherwise sustains. Laib's pollen works, begun in 1977, are also fragile; in fact: "The pollen is the most fragile, the most temporary, but the essence of life of the plants, like the milk for animals and human beings."[13] (FIG. 5) For these works, the floor provides a place of temporary stability, yet the edges remain open and porous, the elements are migratory, the boundaries uncertain (FIGS. 6, 7). Laib captures this material for a short time as a work of art, framing it for us to experience, containing it "in a very abstract environment in order to experience it in the most authentic way," because he wants "to have this very intense, concentrated experience with the milk or with the pollen … a real concentrated experience without any distractions, nothing else."[14] With his "Rice Houses" (PLATE 4), begun in the following decade, Laib takes a fundamental foodstuff and places it in small piles around a marble house-shaped element. In the related "Rice Meals" series (FIG. 8), he fills geometric containers; these brass plates, while abstract in form, are also referential to a way of life that joins the spiritual with the mundane, as they point to rice both as an offering to diners at the table and to spirits in the temple. With such compounded meanings of form and material, and through processes that evoke ritual practices (the pouring of libations of milk and honey or offering rice), these works are more objects practiced than sculptures made.

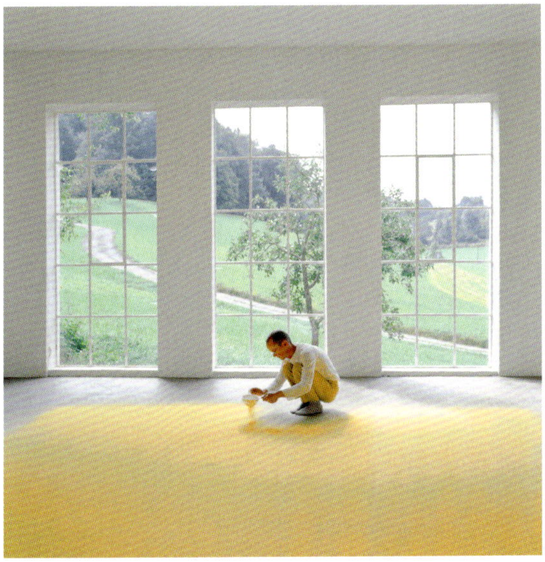

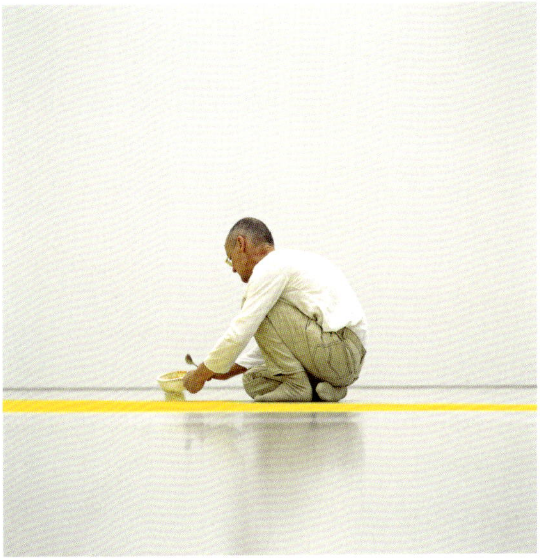

FIGURE 6
Wolfgang Laib. Laib sifting *Pollen from Pine*, 1989. Installation in the artist's studio.
© Wolfgang Laib. Courtesy of the artist and Sean Kelly Gallery, New York

FIGURE 7
Wolfgang Laib. Laib sifting pollen, 2003.
© Wolfgang Laib. Courtesy of the artist and Sean Kelly Gallery, New York

The experience of making is a part of the flow of life, and a way of focusing on what nature, as well as human life, does: "If I sit in a meadow and collect flower pollen, then it is not some philosophical structure I erect. It is at all times the reality, a reality that is so open, so indescribable, so free, and so exciting."[15] To share these experiences and to offer them as an experience to others is both a goal and a necessity. "I was so struck by these things ["Milkstones" and pollen works] because, for me, they were the most important things in the world, and I wanted to show them from the beginning to as many people as possible. It would have been sad for me to have them only for myself. It was like a message. I found the pollen and the milk to be so world-moving, to be culturally important. It's something very beautiful to have this experience collecting pollen for myself, but then on the other side, I wanted many other people to participate in this."[16] The response we have to a work's presence, however, depends on our past experiences. Laib initiates the process but he also trusts that the profound meanings that simple forms and living materials hold can unfold when we bring an intensity of focus to our viewing: "It is all about, for example, simply looking at the milk in the milkstones, experiencing its presence and thinking about it, where it might lead us, and what it might mean at this moment. To feel what an openness such an experience can evoke—this is what I find decisive."[17] "The power of art lies in striking a completely open path."[18]

To have such an experience, there needs to be openness: an opening of time to be with the work, an open space in which the work can be experienced without distraction, and, most of all, an open mind on the part of the viewer. The artist gets us part way there with works that, irrespective of scale, have a sense of infinite dimension. So more than bringing the reality of his materials to art, Laib's art moves us to the realm of the real. It is the real—our being in the midst of the real—that gives this work its presence. So his work must be experienced actually, physically, with the senses. Because these works exist for a short time, they possess a great intensity—the experience takes on a greater sense of urgency, necessity. Their fragility as temporary gestures, brought into being through exacting, demanding labor, gives them gravity and power. In his works' presence, the commonplace becomes mysterious and takes on a presence of form akin to the spiritual objects of the cultures he so admires. It is a presence that is real, yet unreal. And even though the elements he uses may be on the scale of a seed, their presence is enormous,

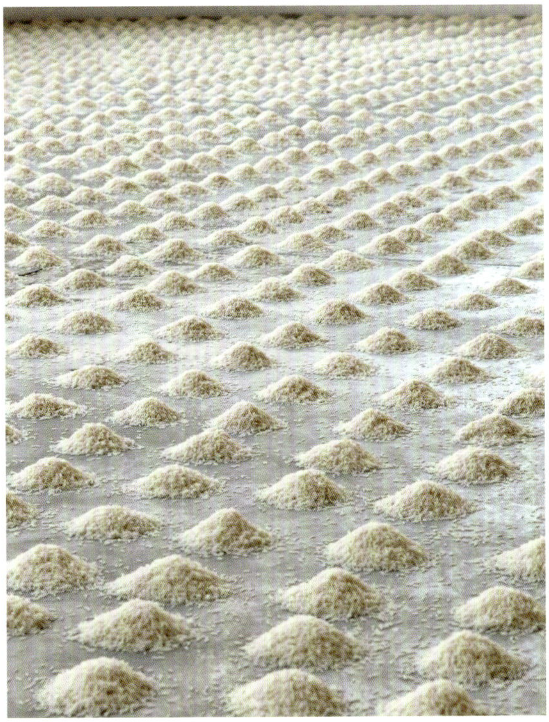

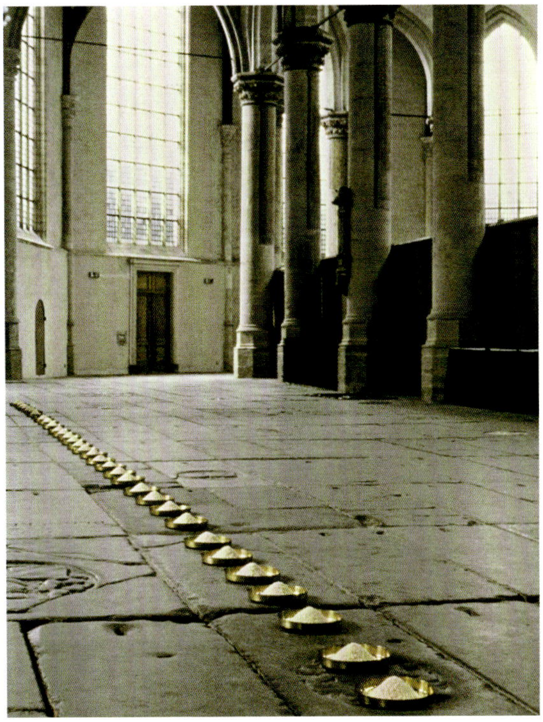

FIGURE 8

Wolfgang Laib. *From me alone all has risen, in me all exists, in me all dissolves*, 2009. Installation at the Fondazione Merz, Turin. About 20,000 rice mountains with 9 pollen mountains and one beeswax ziggurat. © Wolfgang Laib. Courtesy of the artist and Sean Kelly Gallery, New York

FIGURE 9

Wolfgang Laib. *The Rice Meals,* 1987. Installation at Century 87, Oude Kerk, Amsterdam. Rice, brass plates, and hazelnut pollen. Length: 36 ft. (1,097 cm). © Wolfgang Laib. Courtesy of the artist and Sean Kelly Gallery, New York

like a mountain. Yet ultimately, this is all connected: sand becomes stone and stones become mountains, and back again. Laib speaks of this aspect of the world that stands outside everyday comprehension but is present with us all the time and in things that are more than they might appear.

While freezing passing time and the ephemerality of materials, Laib also pursues an age-old desire to create in a permanent way and on a monumental scale. He understands this "permanence" is relative, yet an attempt to partake of something bigger and confront eternal time. It had led this artist, known for his intimate, fragile works, to take on a massive project that is both a work of art and a mountain—both aspects united yet dissolving at their own rate of speed, existing together only for a time. This work, *Without Place, Without Time, Without Body* (FIG. 10), is a wax room, created by the artist inside the mountainside of Le Massif du Canigou in the Pyrenees—a landscape that, to him, "represents a measure outside of time and outside of place."[19] After completing this project, Laib thought about going on, doing similar works, perhaps in different forms around the world that "would give rise to a number of places that are at peace in themselves and yet linked to one another, far from the hustle and bustle of the exhibition world. I'm thinking about different chapels and churches that someone like Giotto made in the course of his life, or the places associated with Rumi or St. Francis."[20]

In the experience Laib affords, he has another desire of vast scope—the aim to heal. This has never been far from his mind. It was his goal in studying medicine, although he ultimately found that addressing the physical body alone was inadequate. "I became very dissatisfied with all what I learned and began to read many Buddhist texts, texts by the Jainas, and began to learn Sanskrit which I continued for three years.... The 'Milkstone' was the direct answer to my medical studies, all that I have seen at the university, all what I have seen in the hospitals, seeing people sick, dying. It is my answer to all this. It was a very deep experience, emotional experience about what life is. And without the contact and the deep influence of the Buddhist texts and of the Jainas this would not have been possible. I am not comparing myself to Buddha, but it is such a similar experience as when Buddha left his home and why he left it."[21] He has been in pursuit since then to find what art can do, how art can approach the problems of life and, re-rooted in ancient wisdoms, can lead

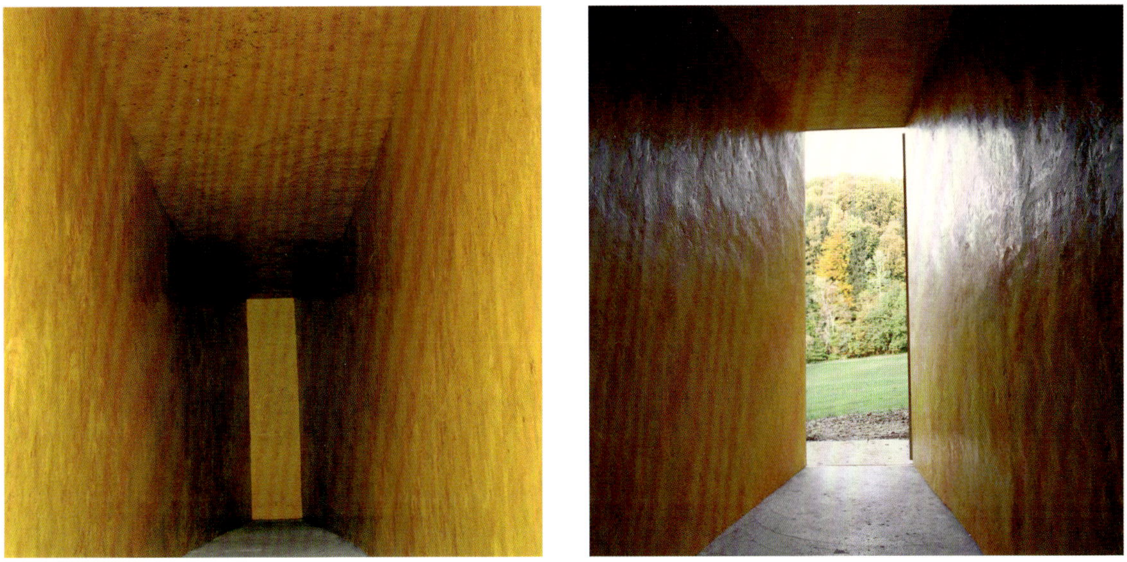

FIGURE 10

Wolfgang Laib. *Without Place, Without Time, Without Body,* 2004. Wax chamber in a hillside near the artist's studio. 11.5 × 2.6–3.8 × 42.7 ft. (350 × 80–115 × 1300 cm). © Wolfgang Laib. Courtesy of the artist and Sean Kelly Gallery, New York

to healing objects in the world. "If art is really good it can include everything. It's the most important thing. That's why I became an artist and didn't become a monk or work as a doctor."[22]

Healing oneself, even for the artist, is the start, and it is an aim perpetually present even as it widens to extend out to the healing of others. Healing is what Wolfgang Laib offers to us and what he aims to bring to us through his art: to have in our life the chance "to think about what you want for your own life, and also what you may want to change."[23] And what the experience of such a work of art does for us, one-by-one, is to transform society. "You can see it from the past: ultimately art and culture, not wars and confrontations, have stimulated change in people ... art and culture have carried mankind further, brought them somewhere else, and it has always been this way. I am still of the opinion that—and this may sound insanely naïve—art changes the world."[24] This change, and the potential to heal the world, is the reason why Laib makes art and illuminates in many essential ways why we look at art. His aspiration is for his art to have a transformative power. From what he puts into these works, we might just expect that power to emerge.

CHARMION VON WIEGAND

To see in a new and deeper way was Charmion von Wiegand's aim in her art practice and in the way of life she chose. "The multiplicity of things which lie in no man's land just beyond the world of appearance enchants me."[1] She was born at the end of the nineteenth century and lived through much of the twentieth; she saw the modern world emerge. Her father's journalism career took the family from the United States to Berlin when she was in her mid-teens. A few years later she entered his field and at age thirty found herself the only female correspondent in pre-Stalinist Moscow. There she met the publisher Joseph Freeman, her husband-to-be, who would later share her interest in Eastern religions. Always the odd woman out, she returned to New York in 1932 to a man's world, writing art criticism for magazines (including Freeman's journal *New Masses*) and, quietly, to paint. Her life and ideas traversed the heights of modern abstract art, and eventually she made her contribution there. But it was in finding a deeper connection to abstraction through Eastern thought midway in her career that proved most important. Toward the end of her life, in the 1970s, she traveled to India, and her audience with the Dalai Lama was a spiritual circle closing.

A belief in a higher consciousness pervaded all of von Wiegand's life; it deepened with time, and became the prime motivation for her art. Of the many sources to which she turned for inspiration over the decades, three were most resonant: Theosophy, Piet Mondrian, and Tibetan Buddhist art. The origins of the ideas of Helena Petrovna Blavatsky, founder of the Theosophical Society who wrote The *Secret Doctrine* (1888), intrigued von Wiegand: Tibetan Buddhism, Hinduism, the Kabbalah, and Pythagorean and Egyptian philosophies. As color was essential to von Wiegand's way of working and, over time, a means of expressing greater spiritual meaning, she sought guidance in Blavatsky's prismatic color theory, and she subscribed to Blavatsky's palette of seven primaries (red-orange-yellow-green-blue-indigo-violet). "Nothing stimulated me like Madame Blavatsky's color scheme. It was symbolic." Later she was even more elated to discover that this color scheme was the color gamut of Tibetan painting.[2] Theosophy punctuated critical moments in von Wiegand's life: her parents were followers and, as it turned out, so was Piet Mondrian—forming a bond in their friendship that enabled a mutual understanding of the meanings of abstraction.[3] Meeting Mondrian was cataclysmic, causing her to see in a new way. Speaking of an initial visit to his studio, she remarked: "And when I walked out of there, I looked at New York and I saw it in another way. It was like a new vision."[4]

She pondered how to embody in material means philosophical concepts that were so immaterial. She realized, however, that to achieve such an end with her work could be "the touchstone for training people to a new sensibility that as yet does not exist even for the most aesthetically trained minds."[5]

To Charmion von Wiegand the greatest realization of this new sensibility was found in Tibetan art. Coming full circle, it was through the Theosophical Society that she came to know the local Tibetan immigrant community and see firsthand their paintings.[6] It was a critical meeting. Here she found not only a wisdom tradition that she could believe in, but also belief actualized in art. Von Wiegand delved full force into Tibetan art, as she had time-and-time before with so many other interests, reading and studying, but on this occasion her passion was even greater, enlivened by her contact with the Tibetan community. On the one hand, she felt as an outsider, "as a Westerner," but, on the other, and more important, she felt a union with Tibetan painting that was "part of the general tradition of humanity. And therefore, you can put yourself into something like that."[7] In 1967 she began a lifelong association with Khyongla Rato, a Buddhist monk exiled from Tibet, and encouraged him to write his autobiography,[8] just as she had done with Mondrian as friend and translator for his writings. And likewise, just as the painting of Mondrian had enabled her to see anew, her experiences with Tibetan art (as she wrote to her friend the artist Mark Tobey) had a profound effect: "Your accustomed points of reference leave you disoriented between the heights and depths, between the beauty and horror—all of it in the painting. And what it does to your view of Western art, seeing it with detachment more objectively for the first time."[9] Later she drew the circle closer, bringing Mondrian into direct association: "I would compare his mentality to that of a Tibetan lama.... Mondrian was an ascetic in all aspects of his

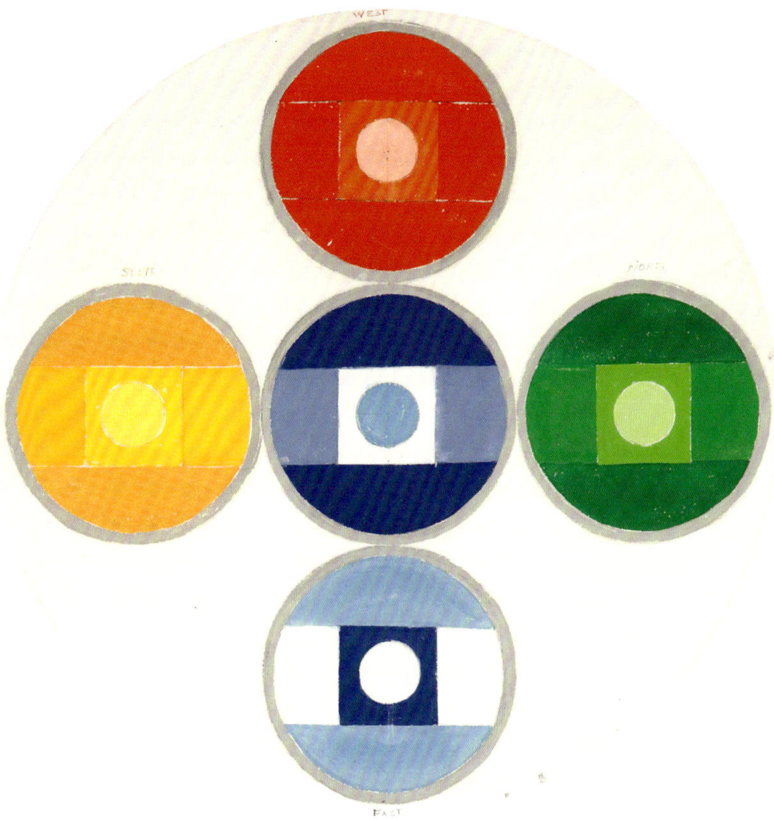

FIGURE 11

Charmion von Wiegand. *Untitled*, 1963. Gouache on paperboard. 16½ × 16½ in. (41.91 × 41.91 cm). Courtesy of Michael Rosenfeld Gallery, LLC, New York

existence. In his life as in his art there were never any extremes. This is the Buddhist way, where knowledge and awareness of all extremes are sublimated and transcended in a new unity."[10]

Von Wiegand developed a strong discipline in carrying out her dedicated love of paint; it was a trait—the focused attention of execution—that she admired in Mondrian; it was a way of working, looking, and being in the moment of painting. She saw how defining this way of working in the studio was not so much about rules, certainly not a formula, but a productive path for the creative process. She appreciated the *I Ching* teaching that "without limits you can do nothing." "So limitation is self-discipline that keeps you within bounds."[11] This enables you to focus, "you really have a section which you work in that is closest to you. Your interior and your exterior meet and that way you can get a harmony."[12] The aim of her focus was to convey a true and deeper nature of reality, to give a form to the immaterial and universal. She remarked later in life that "painting deals with plastic reality which is based on this world. And if you don't follow those principles you can't express the inner worlds, because it's too amorphous then; it disappears."[13] She admired that through pure abstraction Mondrian had achieved: "not the creation of another reality but of another vision—the true vision—of reality."[14] And in this, to von Wiegand, Mondrian had come close to the idea of emptiness in Buddhism: "not the nothingness which the West assumes it to be, but the shining Void of the life source which is beyond name and form: the great livingness in which all duality comes to rest. Mondrian's art is a confession of faith in man and in life: plastic interpretation of the life principle in action."[15]

Studying Tibetan art allowed von Wiegand to take her experience with abstraction further. She expanded her formal vocabulary, adopting aspects of symbolic geometry as expressed in the representation of the chakras, mandala, and altar forms. She incorporated the Tibetan concept of Yab-Yum, which she wrote, "symbolizes the union of wisdom (which is feminine) and compassion (which is masculine) and leads to right action."[16] It offered her a way to visually convey the life principle of duality attained in the uniting of opposites. Color was always von Wiegand's passion and this, too, was amply satisfied in her experience of Tibetan art that, for her, possessed the color of the energy, color as negative or positive, symbolic, oppositional, and like no other art she had encountered—"an intensity like I guess we don't know anything so intense in its

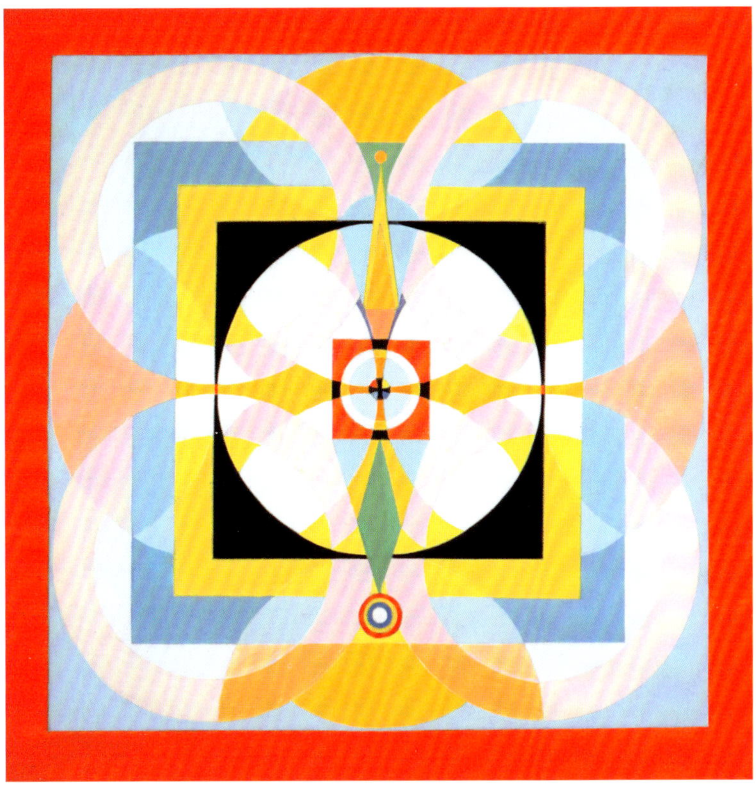

FIGURE 12
Charmion von Wiegand. *The Kundalini Lotus*, 1968–69. Oil on canvas. 35 × 35 in. (88.9 × 88.9 cm), signed and dated. Courtesy of Michael Rosenfeld Gallery, LLC, New York

color and its expression, it's transcendent."[17] It changed her work; "it changed the form and it changed the color."[18] Finally in the art of Tibetan Buddhism von Wiegand found a path to bring together the intellectual and philosophical, the emotive and eternal. The Tibetan path to enlightenment was, for von Wiegand, a path to making art that could embody spiritual belief and work by which she could realize the life she had always been seeking. It gave a unity, "the unity of art," and "your capacity to make a unity of art—is to take that individual experience in life and at the same time to take a larger aspect of it which is universal and you bring the two together and it clicks. But it doesn't always happen. It happens intermittently. And then you have periods where it seems to, when you seem to be working in a direction and it just flows."[19]

Modern art is a personal pursuit, yet intrinsically a product of its time, emerging from and responding to the existential dilemma of modern life. The year 1945 saw a war won but at costs, leaving science and technology in an ethical crisis, what Joseph Freeman called "the moral choice."[20] That year von Wiegand observed that people today "don't believe the problem of our time can be solved by politics but only by facing moral, human, and spiritual issues."[21] Equally engaged intellectually and politically, Freeman urged his wife to join him in a search for more knowledge about the world's contemporary religions, and they set off on a course of study, readings, and lectures. This desire to shift their thinking and find a new perspective or understanding seemed to them a critical need in the postwar period, and it was shared by others who also looked to other realms, traditions, and continents. In this the East played a key role.[22] Theosophy was one route that von Wiegand reengaged; its unifying thought had appeal as a way to make a coherent whole of a world turned upside-down, and the Theosophical Society provided her and her husband with the opportunity to hear lectures on Hinduism and Buddhism.[23] So while some pursued progress as the ramping up of production and greater access to material goods, von Wiegand and Freeman, among other intellectuals, looked to rebuild a world in which progress could be achieved through the transformation of the inner self and one's understanding of the interdependence of all beings. Moreover, von Wiegand reflected on what art can do to advance society.

Though by the mid-1950s von Wiegand had lost faith in politics, she could affirm that: "it is not necessary to become cynical but rather more compassionate toward human beings."[24] In this aim she found Tibetan art to be a model. It provided solace and a path forward, she saw, for the Tibetan community, so brutally turned out of its homeland, that she came to know personally in the 1960s. Tibetan art, von Wiegand wrote in 1969, "has the ability to heal the opposing forces of our culture. It is a magic instrument deliberately designed to destroy ignorance and transform consciousness, to bring one face to face with the reality underlying the world of appearances."[25] She experienced how in this culture art played a role, offering compassion, helping and healing oneself and others—and she dedicated herself to that mission. Art "makes people live better together and gives radiance to life," she said. "But it isn't religion, because art always has one foot on the ground, on earth and may reach for the heavens but the minute it leaves the earth there isn't any art because it is ... a material thing we've done with the hands and it's a bridge between heaven and earth. And that's very important."[26] Clarifying this further, she said: "The artist tries to unify these two things."[27]

Charmion von Wiegand devoted herself in the last twenty years of her life to studying—and looking deeply—at Tibetan art. It told her a lot and from it she gained much knowledge. In her 1969 *Tibetan Art* catalog, von Wiegand wrote in loving detail of the manner in which altars are practiced in Tibetan households, in "every home," and she made a household shrine the focus of the exhibition. From about 1950 until her death in 1983 she also kept a shrine at home. In those last years, when she was ill, Khyongla Rato returned her favors by his care of her. She, in turn, bequeathed paintings to him and the Tibet Center he had founded. "An artist is never really truly a religious person," she had said.[28] But Tibetan art had taught her, more than anything, that art and life join in a spiritual pursuit, and then with her art she could offer to others compassion, a sense of wholeness in life, and a glimpse of a transcendent way of being. "I think of art as being a way of life. That is I think an artist is sort of born with that—to see life as an artist. And once you see it that way it doesn't matter, you may not paint, or you may not travel, or you may not read, or you may not have to earn a living at times. But the way of ... seeing is what makes the artist. And that grows and ... it becomes more part of you."[29] And what the artist does, this artist did, gives the viewer a new way to see and to be.

SANFORD BIGGERS

From South Central LA to Harlem, Chicago in between, and sites much farther afield, place plays a critical role for Sanford Biggers. A strong and pulsating current of spiritual traditions, which in spite of their disparate origins, resonates for Biggers, who finds in transcultural strains a way of contemplating his place in the world. It is a process of syncretism, and the key is to recognize the connectedness when it appears—to be able to see something in different parts of the world as an expression of a shared spirit. For that reason Biggers has gravitated to using simple geometric shapes and forms mathematically determined and of divine proportion, which hold meaning across cultures. "I wanted to create more metaphorically and symbolically, exploring how symbols operate within the mind and the visceral affinity humans have for symbols. This comes from an interest in, for lack of a better description, the sacred societal approach of using symbols and coded geometrics to speak to the inducted."[1]

These connections are revealed *if* you are awake. For Biggers this is a matter of attention and not coincidence. He emphasizes intuition and takes this as far as he can. "Intuition is being open—open to receive, and listen, and sense things that are around you, and see how they can go through you and inspire you, or how you can project back out and continue that continuum of energy or sensory exchange. I know it sounds very New Age-y, but it's actually a huge part of my practice."[2] This year Sanford Biggers followed his intuition to Brazil; he knew that Brazil would be important to him, even though he had never been there, because of its cultural complexity. "There are few places in the world that have all these cultures coming in and mixing and fusing, either blending or not blending: New Orleans, Istanbul, South Africa, Bahia." Energy, as shared among cultures, is essential to Biggers's way of making art and thinking; it's an energy that drives his art. Most of us are bouncing around through energy: "We're not reading it; we're maybe not going with the flow." So a dense and profound experience of energy is one of the things this artist gives to viewers.

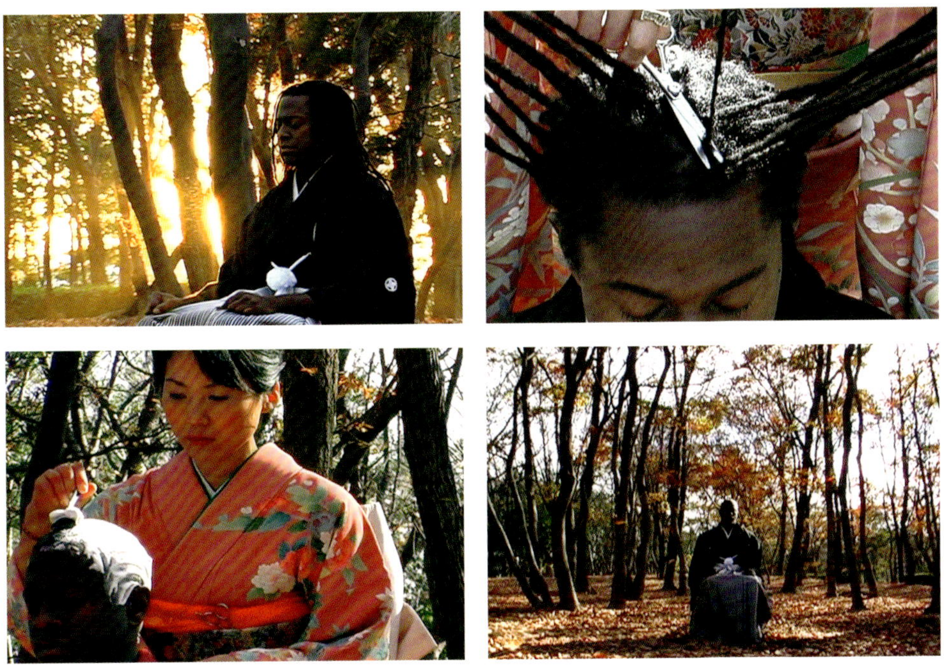

FIGURE 13

Sanford Biggers. *Danapatsu*, 2004. Color, single channel DVD with sound. 8:03 min.
Video stills from original hair cutting ceremony. Filmed in Ibakari, Japan. Courtesy of the artist

During his first trip to Indonesia in the 1990s, Sanford Biggers encountered the gamelan. He fell in love with this musical instrument as well as the way it is embedded in the culture: "It's the sound, the rhythm, the dissonance, how it's very different from the Western chord range and, like African-based music, based on polyrhythms and is percussive. Ordered but abstract and geometric, abstract but not improvised." Since then he has created several projects with gamelan groups. "When I find a syncretic link between my own culture and another, I want to bring them together and see what their offspring will be: I think there is a 'universal vibe' that connects us even if we never have the chance to meet. We often think, feel, and work on the same level as many others despite our physical separation."

An example of this syncretic way of creating art goes like this: "I did performance with a gamelan troupe, with a video mash-up that I made, and a DJ who did an intro of soundscapes that blended into the gamelan performing that segued into the video. The video had a matching audio that at some point dropped out and I started doing psychedelic stuff to just the imagery; then the audio came back in and the gamelan started again to the soundtrack.... And I'm standing there orchestrating the video recorders, the DVD player, the DJ, and the gamelan group. It's the fusion. It's my interest in African culture, then African American, then European, and then global." And here, as in many of Biggers's performative works, collaboration is added to the mix. He sets up the framework, orchestrates elements, then lets them go—"I'm open to these things happening, and because I rely on people's talents, I am open to the energy of others."

In his ongoing search Biggers first found a cultural connection with Japan, and there, the suggestion of Buddhist practice. While he can locate his initial experience of Japanese culture growing up among ethnic communities in Los Angeles, it was a trip to Japan in 1992 that had a strong impact on him. Yet even then, it was more than a decade before he would begin mediating, testing Buddhism as a life practice (FIG. 13). He was attracted to the creative potential that could come with meditation—the chance to open further those channels by which he could receive inspiration from various sources—and then through this practice digest and integrate these experiences. He came to appreciate the grounded frame of mind that comes when meditation is a regular practice, how it can be regenerative, and he came to see it "more of a life way, a way of living and being."

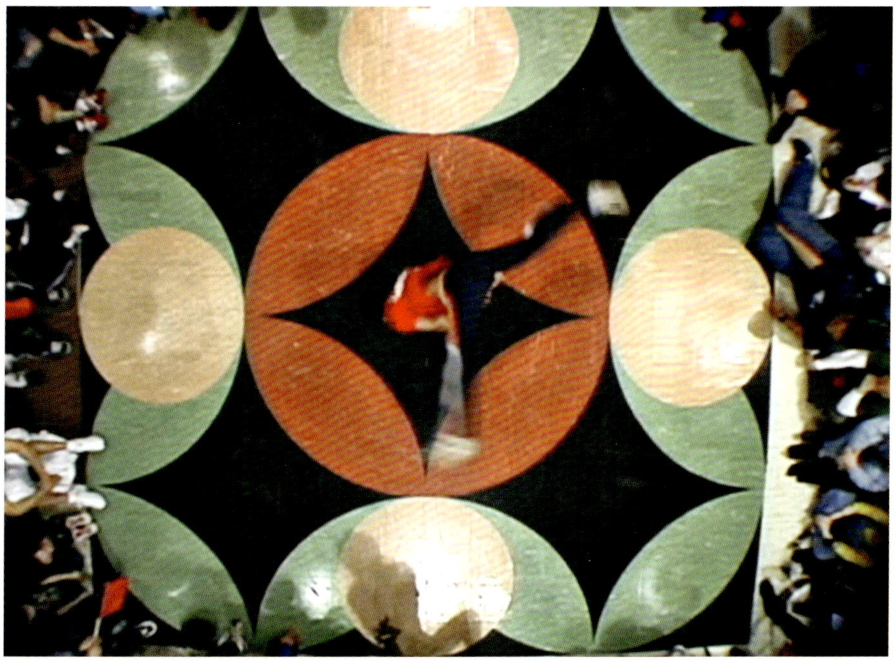

FIGURE 14
Sanford Biggers with David Ellis. *Mandala of the B-Bodhisattva II*, 2000. Hand-carved colored tiles. 16 × 16 ft. (487.7 × 487.7 cm). PS1 Clock Tower, New York. Courtesy of the artists

"When I first started to read about Buddhism, I would attach myself to certain precepts, like, okay, I'm going to focus on that right now. But now I want to go back and read again, because I think I'll read and understand it in a totally different way than I did almost ten years ago. I think I'm open to receiving some wisdom from there right now." Yet Biggers muses on the life of the Buddhist monk: "I'm not sure that I could actually maintain that, though *actually*, there are European monastic practices that I am attracted to, not for the structures of those religions, but the way that monasteries and friaries work. I probably *could* do and find some type of equilibrium and sustenance from that environment as a life force—for a time." A sense of equilibrium and creative energy comes together for Sanford Biggers in the process of art making. Making art can be an act of meditation, a state of concentrated focus and awareness that rests at a depth beyond everyday experience. "When I'm working and in a very process-filled moment, I am totally gone—in the void—and I'm not thinking about anything. I'm just clear. It's very centering and grounding."

To bring focus and potentially depth to the experience of others, Biggers often seizes upon temporality, producing works that demand the conscious participation of the viewer. They also provide an experience with the real. "The fourth dimension is maybe the most immediate way we have to manifest energy. There's a life there." So the viewer has to be present to make the work of art live—to be present in the moment. Biggers admits that art-as-objects let us off the hook, "because we think, well, that will always be there, and it can do it even if I'm not doing it, or I can come back to it." So he often shifts strategy and chooses performance, because "the performative moment frames time. We're able to focus ourselves in a different way—and I like that idea of my art being used as a mechanism to channel focus." This first took form with his mandala-shaped dance floor, *Mandala of the B-Bodhisattva II* (FIG. 14), a work meant to be practiced. An expression of African American hip-hop, he drew from this dance form's roots in the spiritual practices of other cultures, and the energy it has generated across cultures as it has migrated around the world and been transformed over time. He melded this into a potent Buddhist spiritual form, the mandala, that is at once a spatial experience in our own realm and, mirrored in the mind, the image of another world to which the mandala can guide us. The artist's aim lay not so much in creating the sculptural floor or even a dance performance but in offering the potential for a total, transcendent experience for the audience participants.

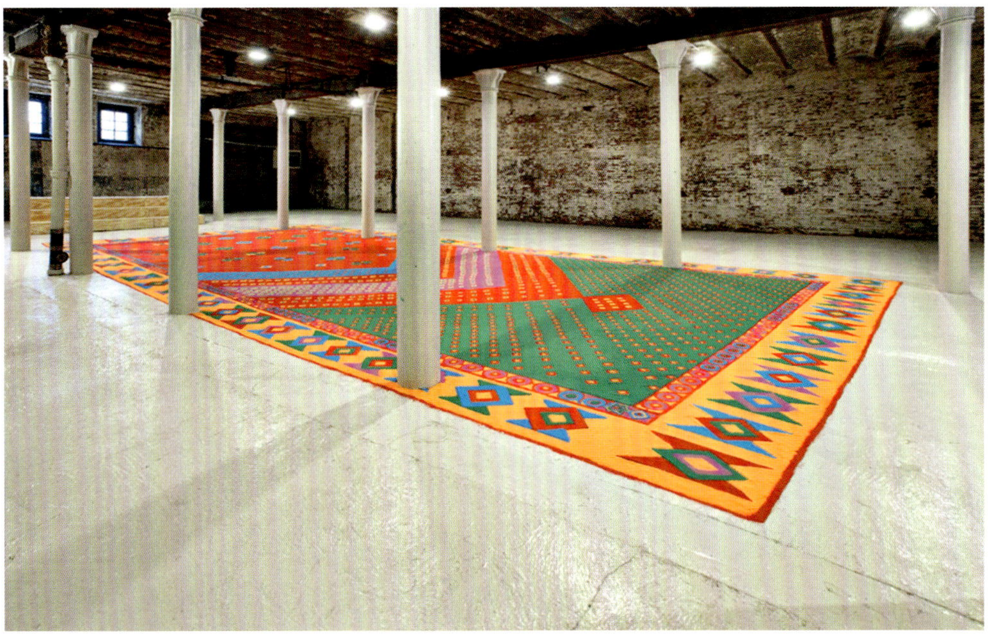

FIGURE 15
Sanford Biggers. *Prayer Rug*, 2005. Colored sand poured unfixed directly onto floor. 40 × 20 ft. (1219 × 609.6 cm). Triple Candie New York. Courtesy of Tom Powell

Seeking to make art that is a part of life's cycle, Biggers desires his works to be a means by which energy can flow. If a sculptural object, it awaits activation by the viewer's presence. If performative, it overtly calls for participation and, while impermanent, the artist imagines its energy continues after the experience is over, and so such a work endures, too (FIG. 15). This is due to the energy he puts into the work and, perhaps even more so, the energy Biggers seeks to tap—energy that is already with us and in which his art, for a moment, like a magnet, consolidates and brings to our attention.

Objects have power. We can feel it in some ritual objects made for veneration, protection, or communication with spirits. "We can experience transcendent works that are very transparent in their intent. You see the energy that went into the making of the piece, the joy or the trauma or the ecstasy. Somehow that is still there." So Sanford Biggers wants his art-making process to not just evoke energetic power but to possess the power, and when that happens, "those are the objects that I think can actually really do something. Those are the real power objects." Those are the works that give a meaningful role to art and demonstrate what art can do as it exists on its own, away form the artist or institution, and in the world. "I come from a long tradition of creators that are motivated from an internal spiritual place. We create from this space and then give that back out to influence and affect other people."[3] Where earlier Biggers felt he was consciously trying to push references in a certain direction, he says: "Now I think I'm more open and really investing more of that energy power into the object itself to see if the object can do the work, if it opens up a completely different door for this person than for that person. That's what I think I'd like to give to a viewer."

The desire to give a meaningful, even powerful, yet open and individual experience to the viewer is grounded in Biggers's own experiences—experiences he has had with objects and observed in how objects communicate and function in other cultures. "It struck me that as an artist, or a creator of any sort, we're not making the masterpiece most of the time. We're lucky *if* it ever happens. But when it happens, all the other works that led up to it are resolved in that one work. The rest is just dress rehearsals and practices, but every now and then, that thing happens. And for me, that's a moment when, it's like, I'm not there anymore. I can register it through

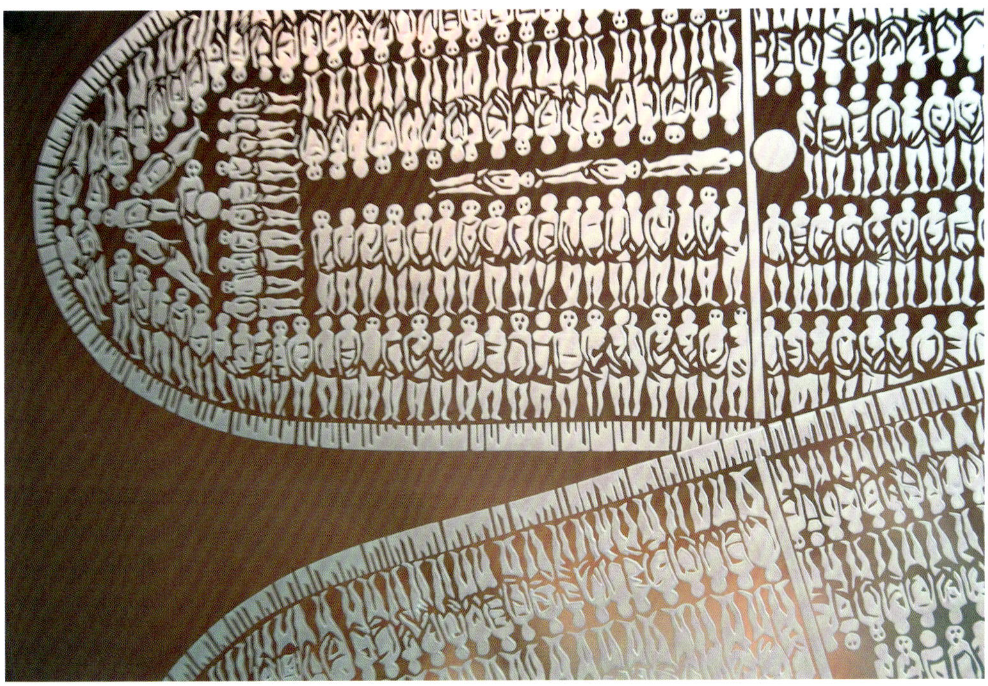

FIGURE 16
Sanford Biggers. Detail of *Lotus* (plate 13)

comments and being around, but the energy resides in the thing itself, not in me. That's one of the reasons I still make work." The enlivened sensibility to which Biggers aspires finds its power in the energy the work transmits, and that resonates within us, connecting us to other cultures and to each other.

A work that no doubt resulted from one of those moments when *it* happened—when things came together, were resolved, and went beyond—is *Lotus* (PLATE 13, FIG. 15). It is a power object that transcends place, though it traces a line through places, over centuries, and across continents. With this work Sanford Biggers takes on the monumental subject of slavery, aiming to manifest a shared responsibility as he confronts the pain of the transatlantic slave trade, so ambiguously and poetically termed The Middle Passage. And he aims to locate and then take this energy to another place, transforming our collective consciousness. The work's image and title reference one of the most basic of Buddhist motifs—the lotus—a beautiful flower that springs from mud and becomes a symbol of the true and good nature of all beings that can arise and be realized through a path to enlightenment. Here the artist suggests that from this horrible history something beautiful is born. Biggers fuses images of slaves onto fragile glass; the delicate etchings of diagrams of slave-ship holds, with Africans in regimented configuration, humans immobilized, form a flowery pattern. It offers a path with its sacred geometry: a perfect circle within which the perfection of images, one after the next, body-against-body. It is both a mandala and a talisman. Experienced on human scale, it reflects back at us, our body impressed onto the many bodies enslaved, while its transparency brings all others in the room into the picture, too. We are all a part of this work. A history becomes apparent and, at the same time, melts away, moving us along while never forgetting. "It's definitely a healing object, an icon,"[4] Biggers offers, adding, "it's about a transitive moment: the idea of taking a symbol of tribulation and turning it into a symbol of triumph; a way of finding resolution through reification and beautification. Maybe there's a new way to look at this experience. Maybe we've gone through all of this now and we're on the other side; maybe this is a way of looking at past imagery and finding a new meaning or a release."[5] That is something that may come with time, compassion, and openness. Sanford Biggers seeks this wide view, knowing that only by locating connections lain dormant a new and transformative energy can arise.

ATTA KIM

Living in both Seoul and New York, Atta Kim is traversing between multiple places around the world these days, initiating a new project, "Drawing of Nature." In a couple of years he will capture the outcome after the world itself completes the work through a process of drawing with its very existence: air on canvas, always there, always changing; each place different, each expression unique, all part of a whole. This is the very essence of Kim's work. Each process he engages is an embodiment of his beliefs about the nature of reality. It is also who he is—"Atta"—his name signifying "I-Other,"[1] an identity seeking completeness, a oneness that occurs when the self is in union with others, and when we understand deeply our own existence in relation to the world.

Atta Kim does not practice Buddhism, but it is a part of his culture. Along with Taoism and Confucianism, he has found that Buddhism has provided a path to a personal philosophy for his life, one that he can believe in and from which he can find a meaningful and beneficial way to make art and share it with others. It is based not on what we see but on what is. "To understand and discern the inner world is a rather important assignment of aesthetics or philosophy of art. I have invested many hours in seeing the inner world of things."[2]

To perceive this inner life, the artist set out a foundation for himself through image training—though, in fact, this is training not just for art making but for everyone to gain greater perception and move toward a more enlightened understanding of the way things are. The first step in image training is to have a conversation, an exchange, with the object of your attention. "The mere conversation is not the point," the artist says, but rather, he shares, "the most important and the most crucial part of focusing on a thing is to open yourself up to something new. Anyone is capable of this, and every object has some quality that we may not be aware of. There are infinite possibilities."[3] This is not a lesson learned, but a life practice: "I've been training for a long period of time and the process has been a blessing. There are worlds I have yet to encounter and these unknown worlds allow me to live." By having, as he terms it, a conversation with an object—by looking deeply—Atta Kim begins to see the energy or life it possesses, and then he can go further still. "That's the case with everything in this world: in the process of doing something, you can see more, find that energy." But there are many obstacles to having such a conversation and "the greatest enemy is what you know, how much you know up to that point," and from this knowing (not just being knowledgeable but being fixed in your thoughts), preconceptions are formed. Then "what you know prevents you from experiencing something new, learning something new. So to find something new in my experiences, there is image training."

Experience for Kim, as John Dewey also understood it, is the process and not the end product,[4] and so it is important to him to be able to experience the process fully in the making of work. So he must meet the cultural elders of Korea who are cultural assets, or take a photograph for many hours, and travel around the world to each city that he considers. "The process teaches me many things toward enlightenment. In the process I learn so much." And this process of making art is personally expanding: "Artwork is just a tool to open my vista." For us, as viewers, the experience is not the same as for the artist; it is not actual, in a place at the moment, and so it is perceived from a distance. Yet the artist endeavors to give us the image of that time and space and, so, offers another experience. "The photograph has its own energy," he says; "it does its own work in the world." Kim recognizes he cannot, nor would he want to, prescribe how this works. "Just as I am one unique person in this world, I want my metaphoric children, my work, to be that way—to have its own uniqueness among things in this world."

To give form to his way of experiencing the world and communicate what he experiences to others, Atta Kim employs photography. He does not use it conventionally to capture the image of an object but rather to show its inner energy, what he colloquially refers to as the object's "background." In this pursuit he has found photography to best approximate the real nature of things. Focusing on qualities of the real in his "Museum Series," he framed persons inside huge Plexiglas boxes, poignantly portrayed Korean War veterans, and brought deities to life, being like a collector, he says, in making his own museum of reality. In the "ON-AIR Project" he embraced the capabilities of digital technology that allowed him to go further: to capture the continuity of time through unusually long exposures and to reveal the interconnectedness of beings by joining together vast numbers of images into one. In this way he brings to the surface more than the eye can see. We cannot hold an image of time in our physical eye and see several moments at once; we cannot see time except in the mind's eye, in memory. Yet Kim can give us a picture of eight hours (the length of the work day) on a city street such as in New York or Delhi, with an exposure of this duration (PLATES 14, 15). He also can evoke infinite time, suggesting a register of ten thousand frames (PLATE 16), and in such views the transience of time is manifested, too, as all beings evaporate from the streets along with the moving vehicles. This is the true nature of all things.

Likewise, in his composite images of faces we can sense what is otherwise not visible to the eye: the relation of ourselves to all others to which we are by genus related and by nature bound. So Kim's composite images are at once a self-portrait and an infinite portrait: self and other. They are a manifestation of the Net of Indra: "Everything in the world is like a net, everything is interconnected and intertwined in this net, and I believe that in our world everything is interrelated. Everything is connected." With such images a totality or oneness emerges as a new "person" is formed from the faces of many. Thus, he achieves a kind of portrait of a collective consciousness—an understanding that we might strive for but which eludes us except at moments when we gain a glimpse of our interconnectedness. Yet it is here before us in Kim's photographs. The artist has said: "One human being possesses an infinite amount of energy, infinite possibility. My work allows that possibility of seeing something that we can't usually encounter." And just as any object can be a focal point for contemplation in image training, so Atta Kim's works are offered to us as viewers to consider existence.

Within the categories of things on which he chooses to focus attention—cities, people, the oeuvre of famous artists such as Wassily Kandinsky and J. M. W. Turner (PLATE 18)—we also see essential differences. In their likeness and unity Kim does not seek to erase or neutralize individuality. "When I make one image from all things, the images becomes formless; there is nothing there. But inside are images and there they retain their uniqueness." Moreover, their individual nature is in constant flux, as we, and all living things, are changing, decaying, part of the flow of time and, as energy, participating in a tendency toward formlessness. Even cities are part of this flow, as his portraits of streets aim to show; each has its own unique energy, always moving and changing; and some will fade way, as will we.

Atta Kim's works do not represent but rather embody the state of things, and this real state is impermanence: "the only reality is change." Thus Kim's practice constitutes an ongoing research into impermanence. It is "about my devotion and effort to redirect and reconfirm the precious value of every existence before its eventual but inevitable encounter with the fate of disappearance."[5] Form is emptiness and the very emptiness is form, goes the *Heart Sutra*. When Kim shows us the accumulation of the whole—in a city street over time, the unity of persons, the sum total of an artist's creative energy—he understands, and seeks to convey, that none are empty. Rather in the nothingness of the photograph, the subject's past, its energy, and its potentiality toward form are all present. "This void," he says, "is really an accumulation of many things that exist in a continuous cycle of formation and disappearance."

Impermanence is the subject of and motivation for his extensive serial works that make up the "ON-AIR Project." Great buildings like the Parthenon endure change over time, yet at some future point in time, it, too, will cease to exist. Kim evokes such reaches of time outside human comprehension when he constructs a Parthenon of one thousand blocks of ice and records its process of melting away. Ideologies are also supplanted, as he melts a bust of Mao Zedong, focusing on four moments over four days, freezing time. Meanwhile the water retained was distributed evenly into glasses. Finally they numbered 108, a holy number that takes on various significances in Eastern religions. "It just happened by chance," Kim said, sharing the astonishing result. Even Buddha melts.

Enacting the end of life through the metaphor of ice melting and form disappearing—*form is emptiness*—Kim reclaimed the water. Its potential energy remains for new form to arise—*emptiness is form*. From the water collected during the "Monologue of Ice Series," Kim grew flowers in an area in Korea that had been recently demolished to build apartment buildings. The loss was a trauma. On New Year's Day in 2006 he undertook a ritual with women who scattered

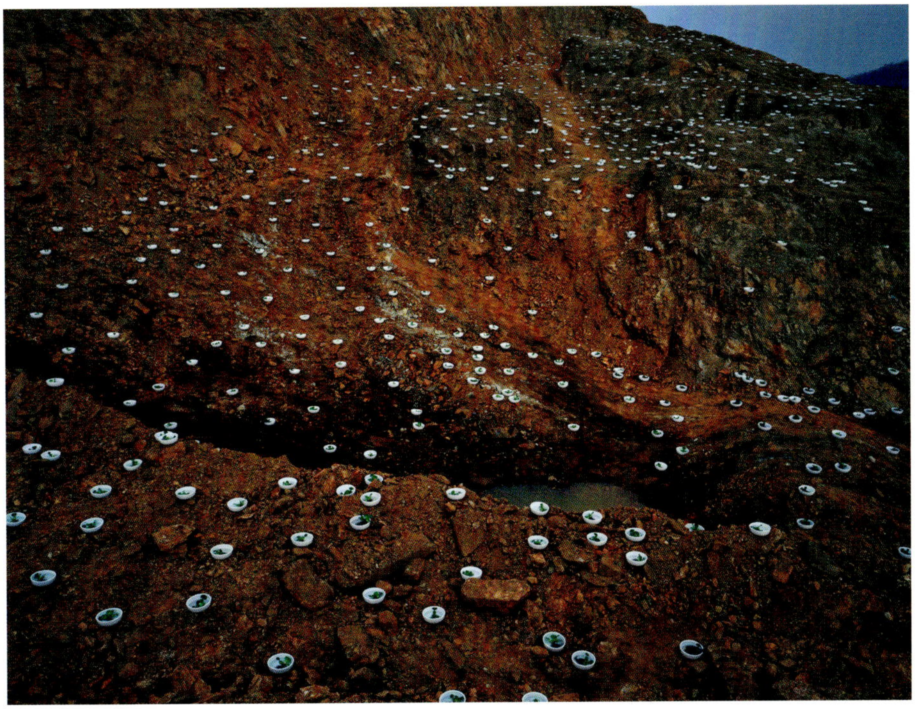

FIGURE 17

Atta Kim. *ON-AIR Project 140, The Monologue of Ice Series, 1000 Flowers*, 2006.
Chromogenic print. 74 × 97⅝ in. (188 × 248 cm). Courtesy of the artist

throughout this denuded landscape one thousand ceramic bowls, each containing the purified water he had collected, placing a candle and saying a prayer with each bowl placed (FIG. 17). (As with his use of the number ten thousand to signify an infinite number in photographing places over eight hours, here one thousand signified the concept of many.) "How can we only count one thousand suffering spirits in the history of human beings?" he reflects.[6] This action recalled for the artist aspects of his childhood in Korea and his knowledge of traumatic moments in history and in his own lifetime. The moment of this act—this art process—was personally transformative. "On the day of the installation, the project members and I performed a ritual to comfort the suffering spirits. It gave me comfort in return."[7] Thus through his own experience of *One Thousand Flowers*, he learned how art can heal and was encouraged in an affirmation of the belief that art can cure humanity's wounds and trauma.

The possibility for art to have an effect of positive benefit on others has inspired Atta Kim to undertake "Drawing of Nature" (FIG. 18). The process is monumental: installing an empty canvas in about one hundred sites around the globe. He is allowing the air, pollution, and whatever elements natural or otherwise to come in contact with and adhere to these clean white canvases—to draw an image of the experience of the place during the time of a year or more, to record its essence.[8] While photographers have considered photography (and other authors have made the argument that Kim uses this medium) to be the best available means to capture the real, with this new project Kim takes it further. "I don't use a camera. I don't use film." It is like a photogram, as it captures impressions. He makes a camera obscura out of the world: when it is dark, the shutters close; and when the sun comes up, the shutters reopen.

The stated aim of this worldwide project is to heal our collective trauma, our wounds, in an ecotopic way. In places like Hiroshima and Auschwitz, he seeks to purify, extracting some of the bad karma by using the weave of the fabric to absorb negative energies. At the Ganges and Bodhgaya (where Buddha found his enlightenment), and in Tibet, where Kim appreciates that there is a profound understanding of Buddhism under threat, he will gather wisdom and positive energetic power. At the same time, joining all these points on the globe, he aims to dissolve boundaries that, as we can see from images taken from outer space, do not in reality exist. Transcending

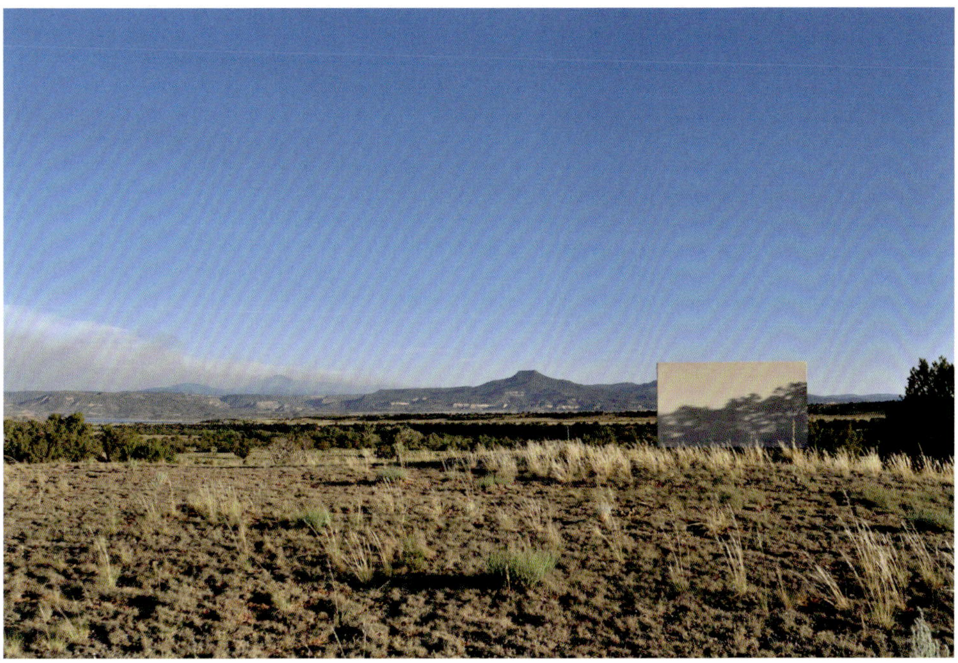

FIGURE 18
Atta Kim. Production Sketch, *Drawing of Nature. Santa Fe, New Mexico, near Georgia O'Keefe's Home (N36° 19'33" W106° 29'47")*. Courtesy of the artist

the ideologies that divide us, this project is, for Atta Kim, a "barometer" of our environment and our shared humanity.

It is important to Kim to share his experiences. "What good is knowledge and your own philosophy if you don't share it," he queries. One takes in, inhales, and so it is natural to exhale. What good is it to gain some wisdom if you can't share it? "That's a beautiful thing—to share it." But the artist also had intention. Buddha sought to understand why people outside the palace gates were suffering; when he gained that wisdom, he knew there was a need to share it, to alleviate the suffering of others. "I believe that this is a very fundamental issue. All things have a reason for their existence; giving and receiving and exchanging is the relationship. If I can't give something back, my existence would not be valuable, and that desire is very great, more so than for most people." But giving back is integral to the natural flow.

This is what is in-progress with "Drawing of Nature." When the canvases return from the many sites to be seen at an exhibition location, they will become objects on which we can train our attention. We can contemplate the past of these places, and most of all, for Kim, our future in the world of the twenty-first century. While he does not determine the ultimate images these canvases will take on, leaving that to the environment, the subject is, as always, the nature of reality. Here the means is the subject, the medium, and the maker. And so the work goes on.

THEASTER GATES

Garfield Park, the neighborhood where Theaster Gates grew up on Chicago's West Side, sounds like a spot of urban green. Certainly that was the aspiration of the landscape architect Jens Jensen when designing this area west of the Loop at the turn of the last century. Times changed, ethnicities and economies shifted, a postwar expressway displaced some families, and after 1968 it became a place forgotten. In a household with eight sisters, Theaster Gates was the youngest child. The African American church and music were part of his upbringing; singing in the choir by twelve, he was a choir director at age fourteen. This was the beginning for him of joining his creativity with that of others. "My job," the artist said, "was to open you up emotionally so that something can go in there."[1] To be open and to engender a state of openness, to open minds, has become Gates's art practice.

Study in Capetown and time in Japan contributed vastly to the formation of his aesthetic vision. Academic studies in urban planning, religion, and ceramics: his approach has always been to follow his interests and perceptions, and then embrace the mix—or even more so—bring them into collision. Yet his aim in bringing domains together, in concept and in practice, is to hone his awareness of connections and cultivate an interconnectedness. It happens in life as he traverses the different social and cultural terrains from West Garfield Park to downtown on the Lake, to the South Side where he now resides. With art as his means, Gates asks: "Can I assert a new way of thinking about a particular geography or a particular kind of person? Can I re-imagine the value of an impoverished life—and not just on some kind of theoretical level?"

Theaster Gates takes from his past experience the power of spiritual music in storefront churches that are embedded in communities and combines it with his understanding of the politics of place and an appreciation of African and Eastern cultural traditions. "I wanted the choir to be able to make and sing songs that addressed social injustices, and not only in religious ways, but in practical and sometimes assertive ways."[2] The act of singing within his projects is real; it is neither the performance of the museum world, nor the performing arts of theater, but a way of being in the everyday spiritual world. "I found that the more I learned about Buddhism and the more I learned about Christianity, the more I saw things as related. And the more I learned about certain kinds of ascetic chants and gospel music, the more I found that they had these things in common, too." In 2008 he formed the Black Monks of Mississippi, an assembly of fluctuating constituency, dedicated to his own syncretic blend of black gospel and Buddhist chanting. "It sounds like church, but a little sparser. And the intensity is sometimes in the silence. So this negative space that started to open up was the result of my imagination about some Eastern aesthetic *and* ascetic."

For *Temple Exercises* (FIG. 19), his 2009 exhibition at the Museum of Contemporary Art in Chicago, he created an installation that recalled at once the architecture of the black storefront church and Buddhist temple, honoring each as a cultural and social marker in their respective communities.[3] In carrying this out, it is no wonder he found his way to the Resource Center and Creative ReUse Warehouse of fellow Southsider Ken Dunn,[4] seizing on wood that in a previous life was palettes in a Chicago Wrigley gum factory. But reclaiming them demanded some care, so their cleaning became another ritual act, undertaken in a manner that would make the mundane meaningful. In Christian terms, it was redemption—redeeming the discarded, reclaiming objects of salvage. But it was also about respecting history, enabling the value that this wood still possessed to come forward, while locating the poetry and beauty of things forgotten. Honoring the everyday by presenting it with dignity is Theaster Gates's process of art making.

This installation and the performances that took place at the museum were only a part of the work. Of critical importance was its role as an index to three places in the city, real places situated firmly in the everyday, and most significant of these was Shine King, a local shoeshining establishment of the artist's youth. There Gates sought not so much to bring *attention to* as to bring the mind of viewers *to attention* as they meditated on others' existence, partaking of cycles of lives lived by people focused on the day's tasks, invested in a way of life that has continued for generations. "It gave me an opportunity to really think about, deeply, for the first time, how did I imagine these labor practices, these brushes with poverty, as a form of dignity or maybe

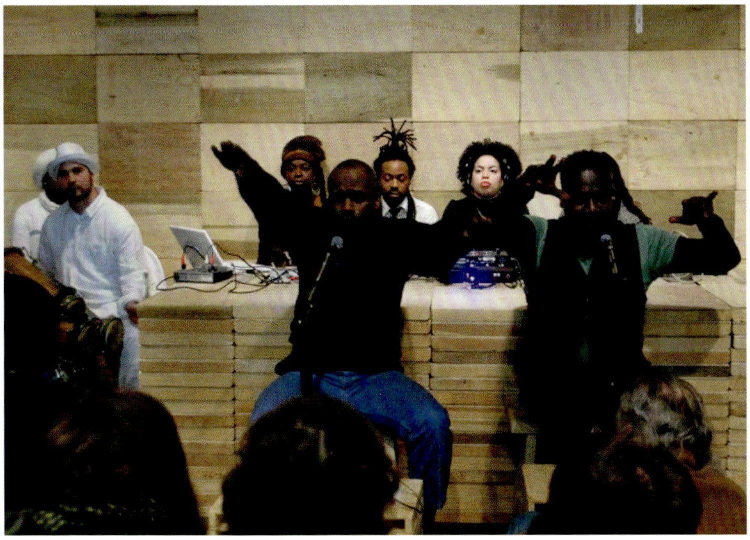

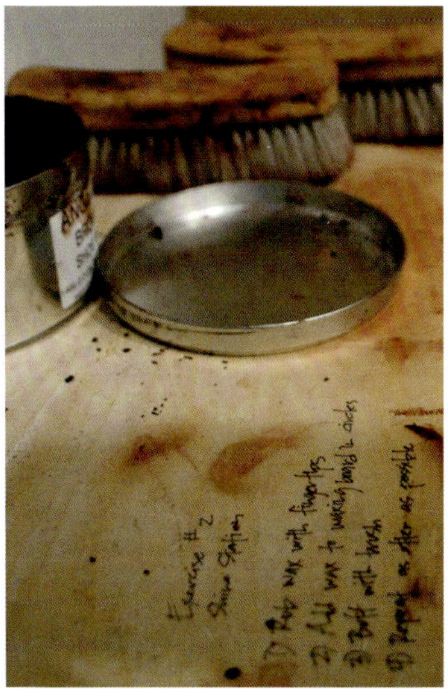

FIGURE 19

Theaster Gates. *Temple Exercises*, 2009. Performance and installation at the Museum of Contemporary Art, Chicago. Industrial wooden boards, found wood, microphones, PA, instruments, and DJ gear. Industrial and non-industrial wood, wax, and brushes. Photograph by Sara Pooley

as a form of emotive monastic labor, urban mysticism." There is a spiritual sense to the word "shining": light reflected and one in reflection, a sense of light and a quest for enlightenment. "There's something equally monastic about the shoe-shiner as a Buddhist priest," Gates said.[5] Shoeshining, sweeping—these are real activities that, when performed with care and generosity, are meaningfully beneficial to oneself as well as practical. So for the artist, "When I say the 'monk,' I'm talking about one who submits themselves to a kind of ordinariness that is seemingly more mundane than what others live everyday from eight to five." And in exposing this to others, Gates understood that those who maintain dignity in the face of economic difference contradict the popular claim that their difference is a deficiency. Reframing such labor in his art making, Gates calls us to emotionally and empathetically share in other social and cultural beliefs and histories that are present in our everyday that, though not a part of our own lives, nonetheless are aspects of the world in which we are all connected.

For his subsequent installation, *Cosmology of the Yard* (FIG. 20) at the 2010 Whitney Biennial, Gates rebuilt his church/temple as the setting for a "monastic residency" of invited artists. Again opening up his museum invitation in an act of generosity, he shared this exhibition platform—and his sharing is always intentional, a conversion of the cultural capital of a high-profile institution into energy, so it can do more. This practice is communal rather than collaborative; those he brings together show side-by-side, forming a small, temporary community, not negotiating co-authorship of a single project. Gates provides a framework, but the outcomes are not predetermined. He depends on the intuition he has cultivated, staying open and comfortable with not knowing what others might do. "I just believe that actively framing these moments is going to create opportunity," tapping into the latent potential of others' energies.

Singing "a monastic version of the chain gang," the Black Monks of Mississippi enacted a rhythm Gates imagined could emerge in the prison yard, while at the same time acknowledging personal rhythms of tending the domestic yard, and occupying the museum's yard. This rather inhospitable outdoor space, however, rewarded anyone who chose to stay there long enough to become a part of this work, to contemplate labor in the humble act of shining shoes, and then to find its resonance in other acts in the wider universe. In this, Theaster Gates's belief in the

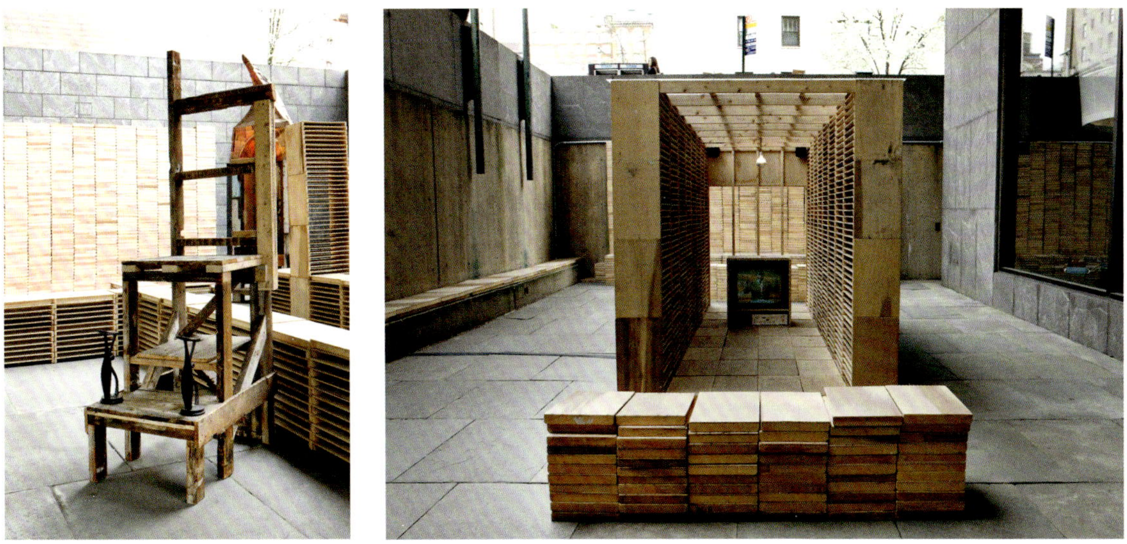

FIGURE 20

Theaster Gates. *Cosmology of Yard*, 2010. Installation at the Whitney Museum of Art for the *Whitney Biennial, 2010*. Industrial wood, shoeshine stand, and video. Image courtesy of Kavi Gupta Gallery, Chicago

value of art as a means of opening up the viewer's mind comes into play. There is a clear intent, and hope, that when viewers go out from the museum, it will be with new eyes and open hearts, seeing the world differently and, likewise, finding for themselves a changed relationship with the world. Ultimately, the communal experiences Gates offers are the means to understand our interconnectedness and the need for compassion. "What Buddhism has given me over the years is this idea that actually my journey is about me, but that my journey can be as much inward facing as it is collaborative, sharing, and communal. And that those moments of inwardness might even inform how I'm a good leader, soldier, brother."

The Black Monks of Mississippi are the focal point of Gates's new video work, *Breathing* (PLATE 23) The artist describes the process of making it: "These four people who had black Christian religious lives, but are maybe not currently practicing, listen to the lead singer's D flat minor, and find the harmonies around that, and just envelop her with a kind of support, so that they could be harmonically connected and not cancel each other out, being next to each other and *sharing* space without *giving up* space." In the end, we experience five individuals on five screens, breathing in synchronicity, and yet, each in their own contemplative moment.

"Buddhism has acted as a kind of guidepost allowing me a more nuanced way to imagine things that I'd always believed in." For Gates it is not a daily practice but a different consciousness of being in the world. He came in touch with Buddhism through making ceramics, first as a student, then visiting Tokoname, Japan. It was an awakening to an aesthetic that could permeate a way of life, consistent with his own values, and expressed formally. This was most profoundly manifested to him through his introduction to the tea ceremony. "This idea that social codes could be carried through rituals that were not quite everyday ones, but were meant to be microcosmic versions of ways to relate."[6] The tea ceremony allowed Gates, on the one hand, to see the value of simple things made well and with respect for nature and, on the other hand, to see how to embed critical subjects of class and politics into aesthetic actions.

Using ceramics, Gates has continued his aim of elevating the everyday—both by rejecting Western taxonomies that denigrate the use of clay and categorize crafts as a minor art and

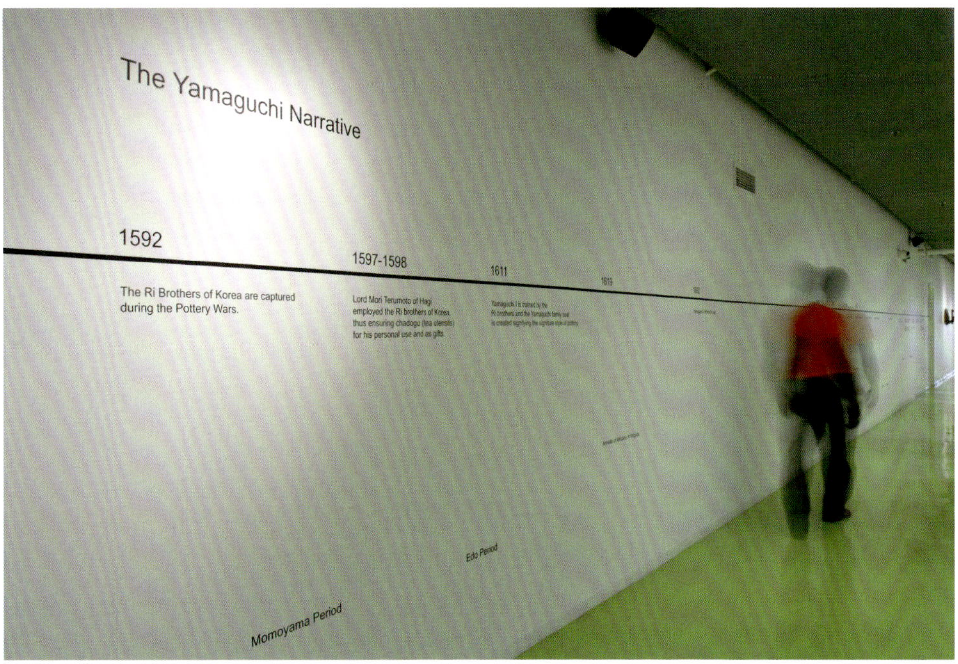

FIGURE 21

Theaster Gates. *The Yamaguchi Narrative*, 2007. Installation at Hyde Park Art Center, Chicago. Black vinyl. 80 × 6 ft. (2438 × 182.9 cm). Photograph by Michelle Litvin

by accepting accidents in the making and decay with use over time not as inferior but another aesthetic code. In the exhibition *To Speculate Darkly*,[7] Gates remembered the African American master potter, known only as Dave, speculating on what he might have felt enslaved in nineteenth-century South Carolina.[8] He also engaged local talents in the realization of the museum show, while provoking more long-term reflection on the social state of Milwaukee. Ceramics, too, is the basis for his ongoing project, the "Yamaguchi Institute," in which he has brought together subjects of Japanese ceramics and African American political activism (FIG. 21). An imaginative use of syncretic storytelling, it became a way to share some painful truths. By creating his own ritual tradition, Gates evokes mythic meals offered on Yamaguchi ware to bridge social divides; now he uses plates of his own making as the platform to converse on life today and change tomorrow.

Social transformation is an aim of Buddhism and can be found overtly in activist strains,[9] but it is also a result of the wisdom gained from practices of deep reflection and contemplation—and in this aim, too, the aesthetic always plays a part. Gates's neighbor of a century past, John Dewey, saw this connection between Buddhism, positive social change, and art.[10] Dewey's eyes were opened by his exposure to this spiritual path during his years on the South Side of Chicago.[11] He found ties between Buddhist philosophy and a vision of the experience of the aesthetic in life; this way of life was, for Dewey, also a path toward participatory democracy dedicated to equality and betterment for all. Like Dewey, Gates is not a Buddhist. "I read about Buddhism. I imagine the practices of people who walk the life of Buddhism as being of value, and reading their biographies is really inspiring. My relationship with the East is more fantastic than a lived experience. Yet there are these influences that I am willing to talk about, that are sometimes passive and sometimes the result of great conversations with great people in another country at a moment in my life when I was open." And like Gates, Dewey was open, too, to these influences one hundred years before.

For Gates, as for Dewey, the keystone is a belief in the transformative power of the art experience to a pragmatic end: art's essential usefulness in building an ethical, better world. This takes the form of creating social experiences that are caring and emotional and strong, like religion

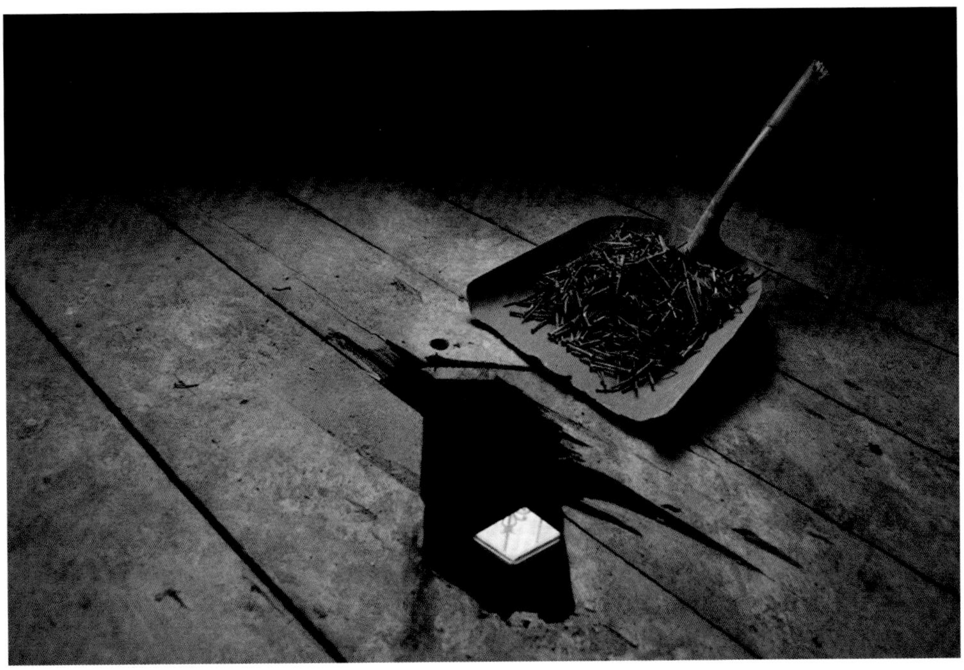

FIGURE 22

Theaster Gates. *Walls Are Down*. The Dorchester Project, 2009. Installation in an abandoned building, Chicago. Broken shovel and assorted fasteners. Photograph by Sara Pooley

and song, and that can open up the conversation to others and open up the way for everyone to think about the questions that face us. "I feel compelled in my art projects to figure out my purposefulness in them—locating myself, and knowing where my tools are and what my purpose is." For Gates this means moving out of the museum and stepping out into the world, into the real. His "Dorchester Projects" participate in the monumental and the mundane. Like that of progenitor-artist Rick Lowe, he seeks to inspire the transformation of a street.[12] But it is not for him to develop land or make a master plan, though he might open space in some minds so that life can be lived more fully on Dorchester Street. He sees the need to have the courage to critique the environment in need of change; he knows that the field of urban planning can benefit from the creative imagination that the artist can bring. "Maybe my practice is ambition," he says. "For every city that went through urban renewal, I feel like I have a lot of work to do." It is physical work and healing work. "When I talk about ambition, it might come out arrogant, but I'm just super-clear about this one thing I'm supposed to do, which is to intervene in this really specific way with this set of skills and these little tools that I have." There are moments for Gates when, with incisive clarity, his work advances; then time opens up. "What I try to do is create these zones where my body and soul get what they need. The most contemplative time is probably riding out the next project, because the next project is telling me how best to use my purposefulness."

For now Theaster Gates owns two houses on Dorchester (FIG. 22) and has use of a third lot. The forgotten things that he has amassed, redeemed, are being turned over for the use of this local community and for others that he knows will come here, too, to use a library comprising of the phenomenal resources on architecture from the former Prairie Avenue bookstore; to peruse an extensive archive of rare, large-format slides discarded by the University of Chicago's art history department; and to help create or sit in a garden that is yet to arise from an abandoned lot. "Led by ambition, slowed down by conscience," he knows with action comes responsibility. But enabled by his consciousness, Theaster Gates builds an emerging center that is clearly a manifestation of the centeredness he aims to maintain, and in which Buddhism plays a part.

Introduction (pp. 25–28)

1 John Dewey, *Art as Experience* (New York: Penguin Group, 2005), 309.

2 Van Meter Ames, *Zen and American Thought* (Honolulu: University of Hawaii Press, 1962), 229.

3 John Dewey, *Experience and Nature and Human Nature* (New York: W.W. Norton, 1925, undated reprint), 373.

4 John Dewey, *Art as Experience*, 359–360.

5 Dewey bemoaned the separation of art from life in museums, especially locating it as a product of the growth of capitalism that "has been a powerful influence in the development of the museum as the proper home for works of art, and in the promotion of the idea that they are apart from the common life." He set himself to address the problem, which he stated as: "that of recovering the continuity of esthetic experience with normal processes of living." John Dewey, *Art as Experience*, 7, 9. But even Dewey certainly saw the potential value of museums being one of its greatest advocates in the twentieth century.

Laib (pp. 29–38)

1 Klaus Ottmann, *Wolfgang Laib: A Retrospective* (Ostfildern-Ruit: Hatje Cantz, 2000), 163. Jakob Bräckle was a local landscape painter who shared ideas with Laib during his formative years; his modest lifestyle was also an influence. The Malevich paintings that Bräckle kept for a friend, Hugo Häring, were eventually acquired by the Stedelijk Museum, Amsterdam.

2 Darren James Jorgensen, "Wolfgang Laib: Returning to What Is" *Electronic Melbourne Art Journal* no. 1 (July/December 2005): 5.1–7.

3 Sarah Tanguy, "Making the Ideal Real: A Conversation with Wolfgang Laib," *Sculpture* (Washington, D.C.) 20, 4 (May 2001): 30.

4 Wolfgang Laib and Necmi Sönmez, "Where Matter Probably Becomes Energy—or Immaterial," in *Wolfgang Laib, Die neun Planeten oder wie die Zusammenhänge auch sein könnten, The Nine Planets or How the Interrelationships Also Could Be* (Ostfildern-Ruit: Hatje Cantz, 2002), 31.

5 The artist said: "It is great if the same or similar thoughts and ideas appear in quite different places and at quite different times—and it is even greater if you, as an individual, are part of a whole." Katharina Schmidt, "Wolfgang Laib—Ways and Works: Ancient Symbols, Recollected in New Forms," in Foundation Beyeler, *Wolfgang Laib: Das Vergängliche ist das Ewige, The Ephemera is Eternal* (Ostfildern-Ruit: Hatje Cantz, 2006): 51.

6 Peter Lodemeyer, "Time—Space—Existence: A Conversation with Wolfgang Laib," *Sculpture* 27, 2 (March 2008), 28.

7 For instance, of collecting pollen as a spiritual practice, he has said: "Other people might think it's a spiritual practice, but it's also something very, very simple and very straightforward. But it's also something else. If you collect pollen from a meadow or in the forest for day after day for one or two months and afterwards you have a jar that's not even full, this is something completely different from what everyone else does. It's even beyond spiritual practice. You don't need a name for it. For me, it's something that challenges everything else: what I do or what I could do." Jorgensen, 1.

8 Jorgensen, 2.

9 Lodemeyer, 27.

10 Dewey said: "Since *art* is the most direct and complete manifestation there is of experience *as* experience, it provides a unique control for the imaginative ventures of philosophy." John Dewey, *Art as Experience* (New York: Penguin Group, 2005), 309. Philosopher Richard Shusterman proposes a somatic philosophy, somaesthetics, based on Dewey, to cultivate "life in the interest of a more intense and just appreciation of the meanings present in experience." See Richard Shusterman, *Practicing Philosophy: Pragmatism and the Philosophical Life* (New York: Routledge, 1997), 21–22.

11 Jorgensen, 1.

12 Wolfgang Laib in correspondence with Martin Brauen, December 17, 2009.

13 Ibid.

14 Tanguy, 32.

15 Lodemeyer, 27.

16 Tanguy, 31.

17 Lodemeyer, 27.

18 Lodermeyer, 26.

19 Laib, 73.

20 Laib, 71.

21 Wolfgang Laib in correspondence with Martin Brauen, December 17, 2009.

22 Jorgensen, 2.

23 Tanguy, 30.

24 Lodemeyer, 28.

Von Wiegand (pp. 39–45)

1 Jennifer Newton Hersh, "Abstraction, Spiritualism, and Social Justice: The Art and Writing of Charmion von Wiegand" (PhD diss., Graduate Center of the City University of New York, 1989), 286. Also see Hersh for an insightful and thorough discussion of the artist's work.

2 Ibid., 29–30.

3 Of Mondrian's relationship to Theosophy, von Wiegand remarked: "One could say that he had gone beyond it. He had digested it as discipline and it had become implicit to his life." Charmion von Wiegand, "Interview with Charmion von Wiegand," by Margit

Rowell, in *Piet Mondrian, 1872–1944: Centennial Exhibition* (New York, NY: Solomon R. Guggenheim Foundation, 1971), 77. + Mondrian officially joined theosophical society in 1909 but even by 1900 had designed a bookplate using theosophical symbols of lotus and hexagram. Hersh, "Charmion von Wiegand," 303, n88.

4 Charmion von Wiegand, oral history interview by Paul Cummings, October 9, 1968, transcript, Oral History Program, Archives of American Art, Smithsonian Institution, Washington, D.C., 17.

5 Charmion von Wiegand and William C. Agee, *Charmion Von Wiegand: Improvisations—1945* (New York: Michael Rosenfeld Gallery, 2003), 50.

6 Charmion von Wiegand first visited the Tibetan community in New Jersey with members of the Theosophical Society; seeing their temple she said: "I was spell-bound—knocked out by the color. That is why my pictures changed. You can't change your color and not your format, so that is why my format changed." Cummings, 104.

7 Cummings interview, 103.

8 Khyongla Rato, *My Life and Lives: The Story of a Tibetan Incarnation* (New York: Dutton, 1977).

9 Hersh, "Charmion von Wiegand," 412.

10 Rowell interview, 86. "Von Wiegand even said to Mondrian of his interweaving planes, 'Well, then you're a tantric artist.' Because the word—tantric—means weaving, I mean you weave a picture." Cummings interview, 52.

11 Cummings interview, 33–34.

12 Ibid., 73.

13 Ibid., 52.

14 Rowell interview, 86. "Mondrian said: 'True abstraction is not rejecting or eliminating parts of the whole of reality, but intensifying it. The culture of art is a continuous attempt to move toward more profoundness.'" Hersh, "Charmion von Wiegand," 307.

15 Hersh, "Charmion von Wiegand," 389.

16 Charmion von Wiegand, "Introduction," in *The Art of Tibet* (New York: American Federation of Arts, ca. 1969), [8].

17 Ibid., 74.

18 Cummings interview, 102.

19 Ibid., 100–101.

20 Hersh, "Charmion von Wiegand," 279. See Hersh dissertation for a lucid discussion of the zeitgeist of the post-World-War II period and its affects on von Wiegand and Freeman.

21 Hersh, "Charmion von Wiegand," 326. Searching for more paths to the future answers, Freeman writes to his wife in 1948: "But it is a hopeful sign that all the sciences today, physics and biochemistry included, recognize that … the material conquest of nature has landed us in a sanguinary cul-de-sac BECAUSE WE KNOW SO LITTLE ABOUT OUR OWN NATURE, AND THEREFORE CANNOT CONTROL IT … so now … the anthropologists, sociologists, and psychiatrists are beginning to discover the control and social atom—MAN. This may be our last best hope on earth—and certainly it is my chief interest today." Ibid., 326–327.

22 At this time Albert Einstein declared: "The religion of the future will be cosmic religion. It should transcend a personal God and avoid dogmas and theology. Covering both the natural and the spiritual, it should be based on a religious sense arising from the experience of all things, natural and spiritual and a meaningful unity. Buddhism answers this description.… If there is any religion that would cope with modern scientific needs, it would be Buddhism." Dr. Martin J. Verhoeven, "Buddhism and Science: Probing the Boundaries of Faith and Reason," *Religion East and West* 1 (June 2001): 77–97.

23 Cummings interview, 25. They also learned about yoga and attended some of D. T. Suzuki's lectures at Columbia University. Cummings interview, 68.

24 Hersh, "Charmion von Wiegand," 351. In 1953 Freeman was brought before the McCarthy The House Committee on Un-American Activities, which had painful affects for the coupe among family and friends. See Hersh, "Charmion von Wiegand," 348–351.

25 Hersh, "Charmion von Wiegand," 391.

26 Cummings interview, 108.

27 Ibid., 51.

28 Ibid., 51–52.

29 Ibid., 99.

Biggers (pp. 46–54)

1 Saul Williams, "Interview with Sanford Biggers by Saul Williams, aka Niggy Tardust," Sanford Biggers, 2006, http://www.sanfordbiggers.com/essays-publications-interviews/interview-with-saul-williams.html.

2 Unless otherwise noted, all quotes are from the author's interview with the artist on May 6, 2010.

3 Williams [not paginated].

4 *Black Lotus* is a 2010 Percent for the Arts commission for a new school in the Bronx. A metal version of this image is on the outside wall, thirty-foot in diameter. A smaller eight-foot version is on view in the United States Embassy in Madagascar.

5 Biggers describes that context has played a large role in siting this work. Of his 2009 exhibition, "Peculiar Institutions," at Solvent Space in Richmond, Virginia, he told the author: "It was minutes away from the docks that were a port of entry for enslaved

Africans. "And the way it was hanging in the space, it was almost like an iris looking out over the river, and it had a little sway, so it was almost like it was searching—just looking, scanning the river." "Now, for me, there are two other places for it to be. One would be in a an underground railroad type of museum very steeped in African American history, and the other is a Buddhist institution, where the mandala and the spiritual side of it could actually be experienced among other objects that have that same type of energy."

Kim (pp. 55–62)

1 Atta Kim changed his name to "Atta": "a" meaning self in Chinese, and "tta" meaning others.
2 Atta Kim, "Is It ON-AIR? Interview with Atta Kim," by Inhee Iris Moon, in *Atta Kim: Water Does Not Soak In Rain* (Ostfildern-Ruit: Hatje Cantz, 2009), 356.
3 Unless otherwise noted, all quotes are from the author's interview with the artist on May 6, 2010.
4 Dewey said: "The process is art and its product, no matter at what stage it be taken, is a work of art." John Dewey, *Experience and Nature and Human Nature* (New York: W.W. Norton, 1925, undated reprint), 373.
5 Moon, 354.
6 Atta Kim, "One Thousand Flowers," in *Atta Kim: Water Does Not Soak In Rain* (Ostfildern-Ruit: Hatje Cantz, 2009), 268.
7 Ibid.
8 The project began in 1994 in Korea when Kim experimented in this way in a forest where he has a studio.

Gates (pp. 63–72)

1 Unless otherwise noted, all quotes are from the author's interview with the artist on June 10, 2010.
2 Rachel Furnari, "High Spirits: Artist Theaster Gates Can't Stop Reaching New Heights," *New City*, March 30, 2010, http://art.newcity.com/2010/03/30/high-spirits-artist-theaster-gates-cant-stop-reaching-new-heights/.
3 Emily Warner, "Theaster Gates," *Proximity Magazine* 4, (May 10, 2009), http://proximitymagazine.com/2009/05/theaster-gates-2/. Of *Temple Exercises*, the artist said: "I really just wanted to build a space where all of my different worlds, these isolated geographies, could come together. And inside that space, I can do what do. And that's what I did: I made a secular scared space."
4 Ken Dunn, of Mennonite background, came to the University of Chicago to study philosophy but instead took up its practical application to promote recycling in Hyde Park, starting in 1969 the Resource Center/Creative Reuse Warehouse, a non-profit environmental education organization, that has led the way in demonstrating innovative techniques for recycling and reusing materials. See "Resource Center: Home," Resource Center, http://www.resourcecenterchicago.org/index.html.
5 Warner.
6 Warner.
7 See Theaster Gates, Jr., *My Name is Dave: A Hymnal*," (Milwaukee: Milwaukee Art Museum and Chipstone Foundation, 2010).
8 Ibid., 48. This nineteenth-century potter active from 1834–62, who dated and signed his ample and beautiful storage jars "Dave," and sometimes adding short poems. Such a practice tested legal boundaries since the education of enslaved Africans and African Americans was prohibited. In an imagined dialogue with Dave, Gates wrote in this book on the image of a pot: "A glaze to match the color of deepest joy and clay of bodied sorrow."
9 See Suzanne Lacy, "Having it Good: Reflections on Engaged Art and Engaged Buddhism," in *Buddha Mind in Contemporary Art*, eds. Jacquelynn Baas and Mary Jane Jacob (Berkeley: University of California Press, 2004), 97–112.
10 The philosopher John Dewey lived at 1554 East 61st Street, near Theaster Gates's current residence at 69th Street and Dorchester Avenue. This was Dewey's home while heading the University of Chicago's Department of Philosophy, Psychology, and Education from 1894 to 1904, during which time he also founded the famous Laboratory School as an experience in Progressive Education.
11 Parallel to Dewey's eight years at the University of Chicago, D.T. Suzuki was in nearby LaSalle, Illinois, where he was working on the first translations of Buddhist text. Later in 1919 Suzuki met Dewey in Japan and served as guide and translator.
12 In 1993 the artist and community activist Rick Lowe inspired saving twenty-two shotgun-style houses in Houston's Third Ward, one of the city's oldest African-American communities. It sparked a successful project, which includes artists' residencies, houses for young mothers, a community gallery, a park, and low-income residential and commercial spaces. It has also grown from the original block and a half to six blocks. In 2003 Project Row Houses established the Row House Community Development Corporation as a separate, affiliated corporation. See http://projectrowhouses.org/about/.

PLATES

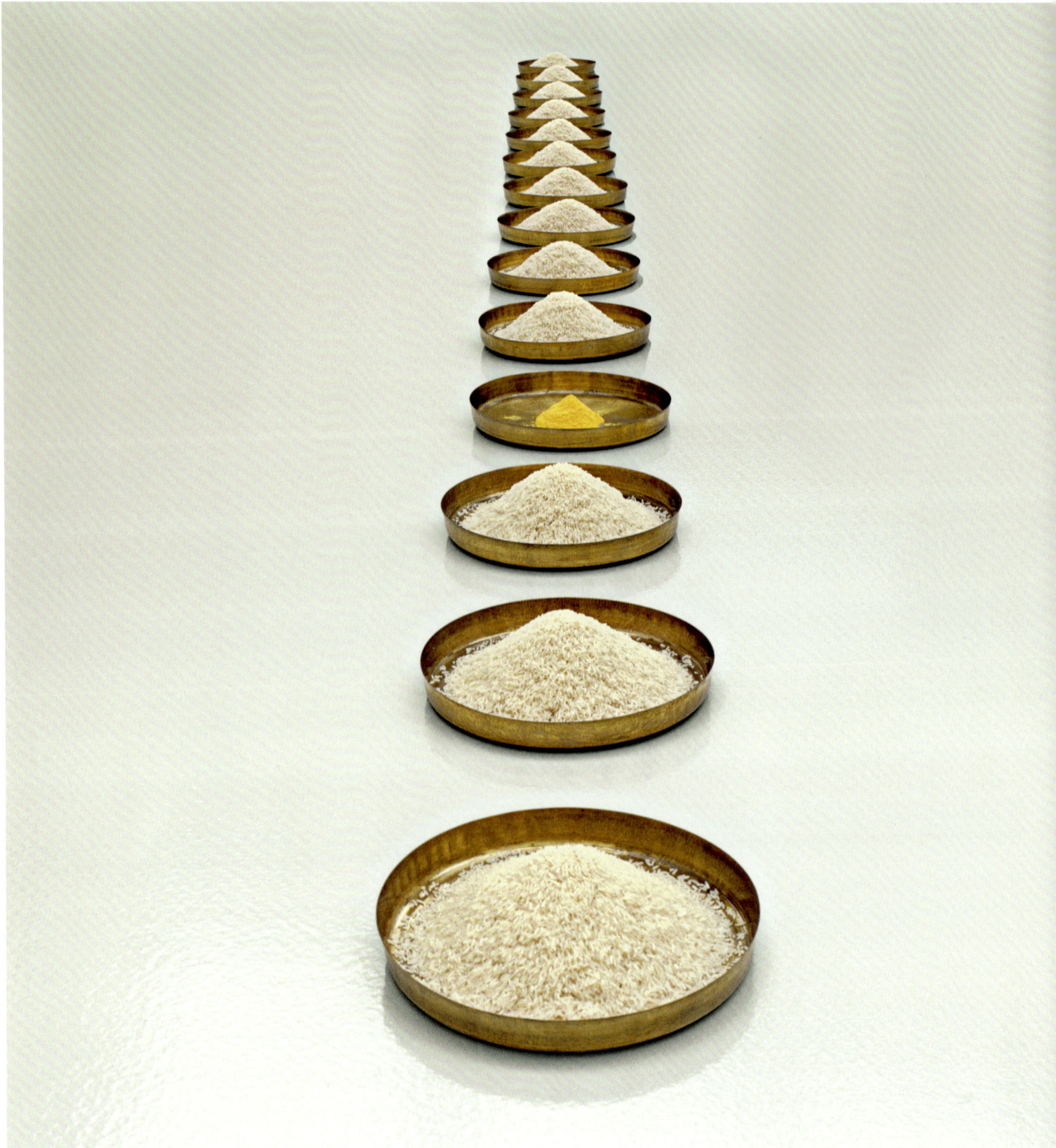

1

WOLFGANG LAIB
Rice Meals, 2010
33 brass plates, rice, and hazelnut pollen
Approximate length: 53 ft. 4 in. (16.26 m)

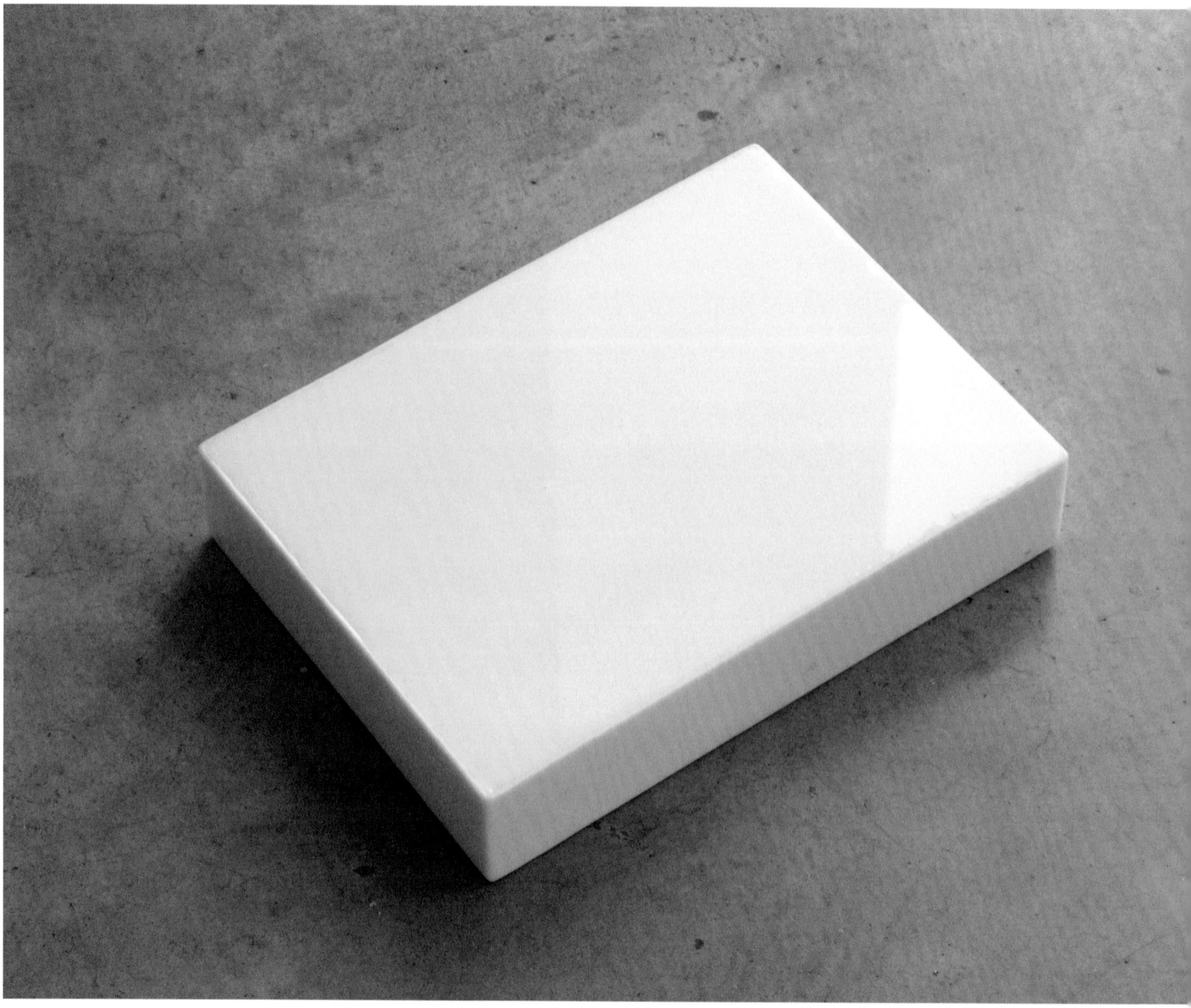

2

WOLFGANG LAIB

Milkstone, 2010

White marble, milk

2⅜ × 20½ × 24½ in. (6 × 52 × 62 cm)

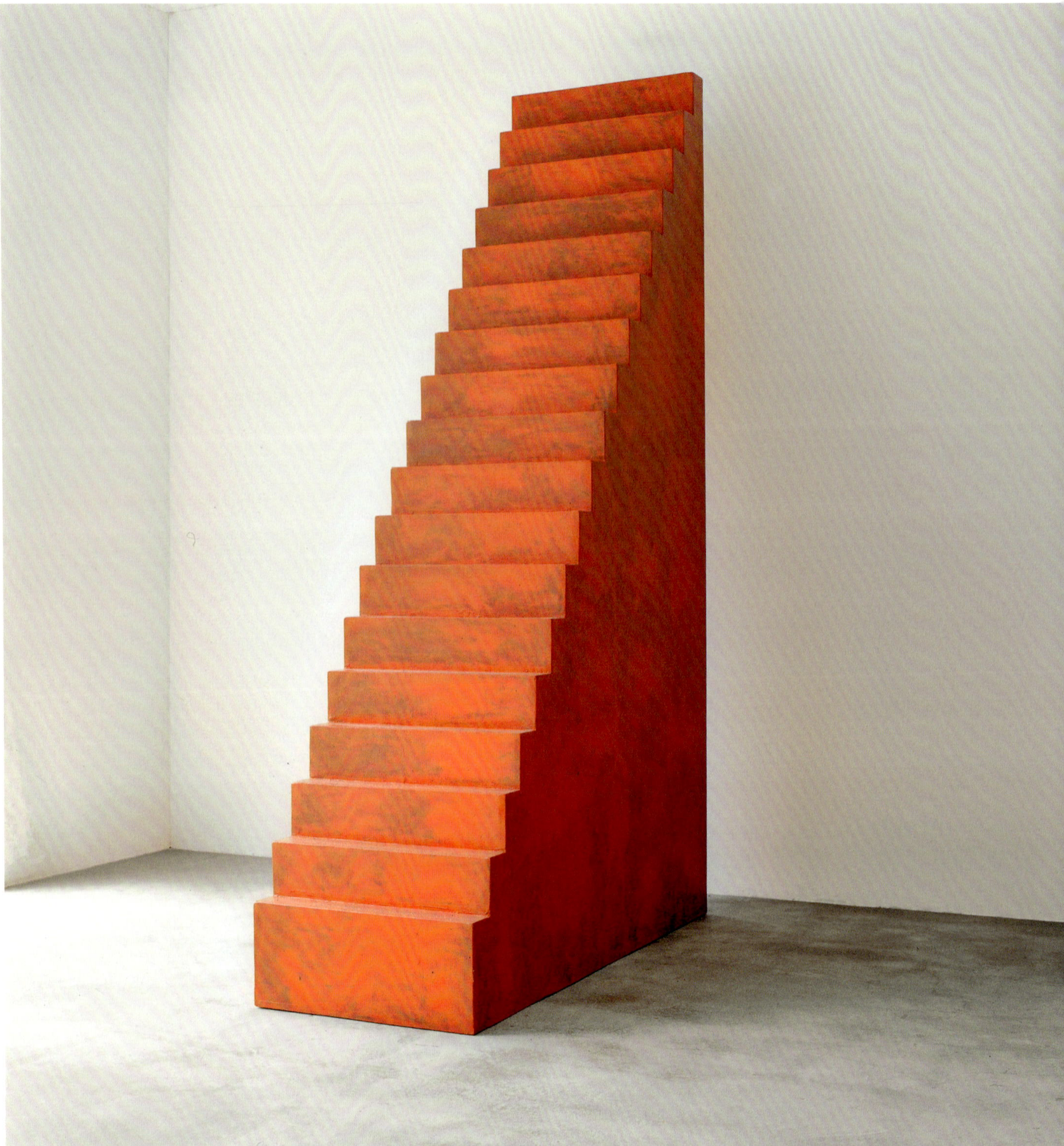

3

WOLFGANG LAIB
Untitled (*Stairs*), 2002
Burmese red lacquer and wood
126 × 29⅛ × 72⅜ in. (320 × 74 × 184 cm)

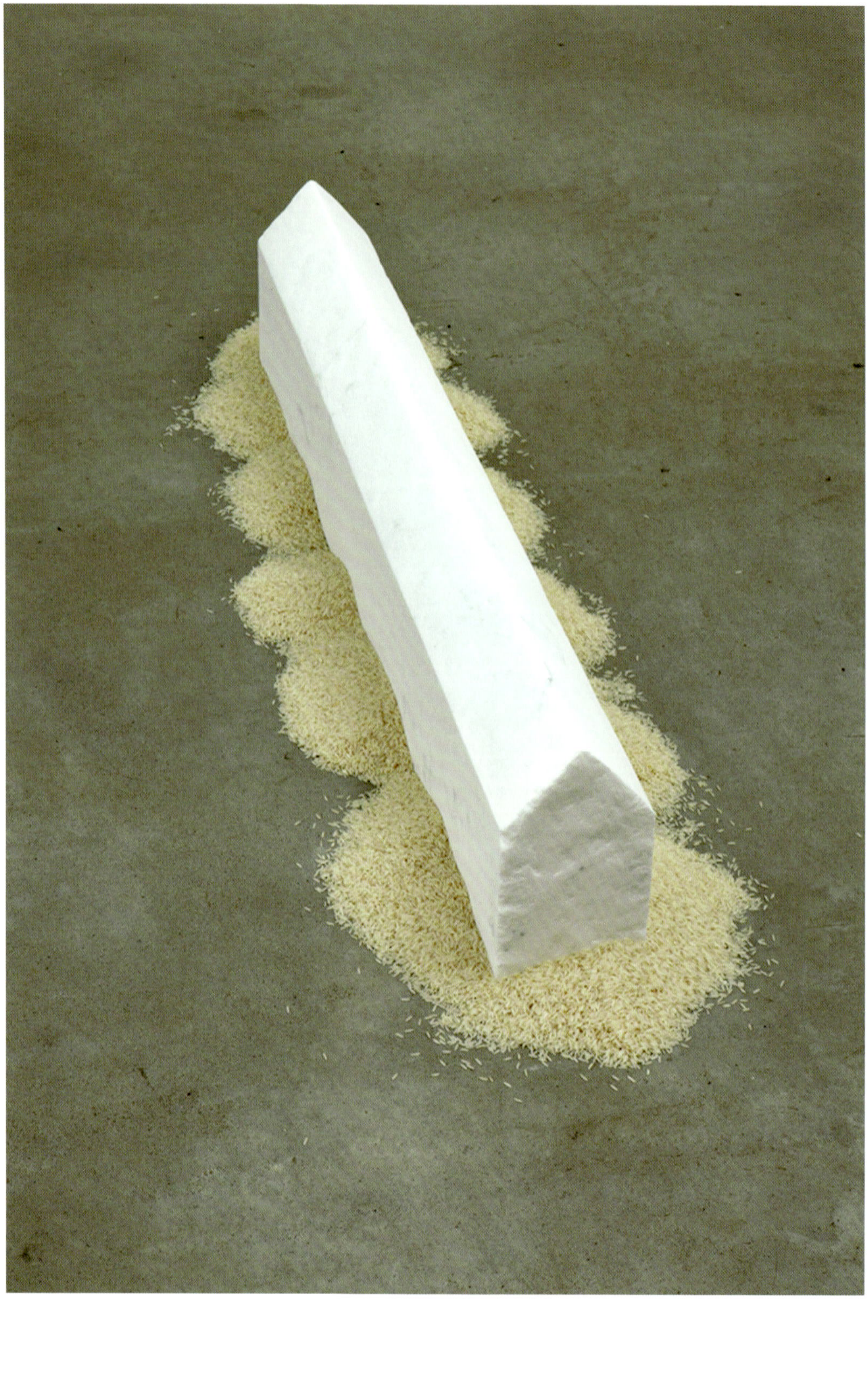

4

WOLFGANG LAIB
Rice House, 2009
Marble and rice
8 ¼ × 4 ¾ × 39 in. (21 × 12 × 99 cm)

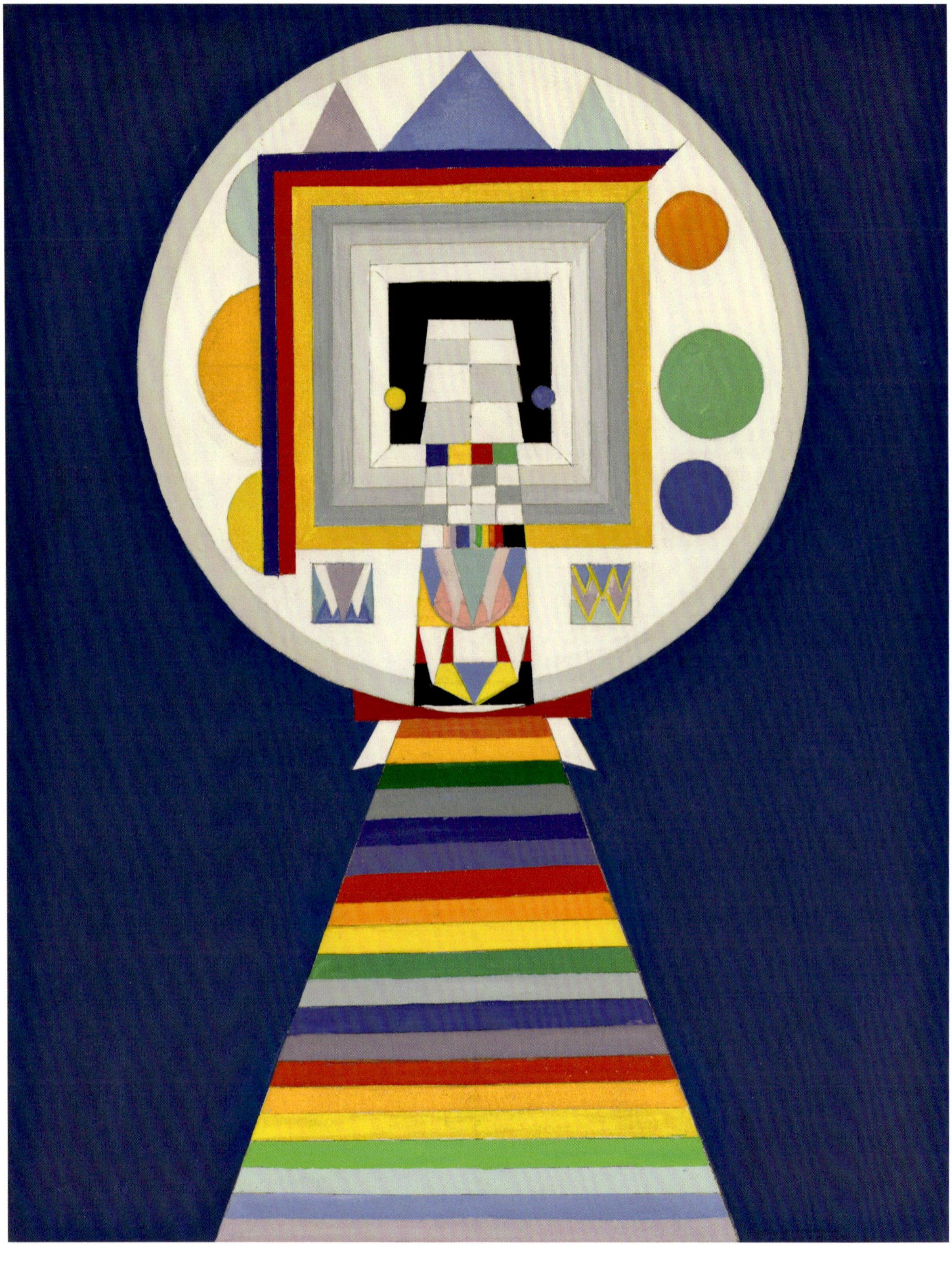

5

CHARMION VON WIEGAND
The Ascent to Mt. Meru, 1962
Gouache on paper
23⅜ × 18⅜ in. (59.4 × 46.7 cm)

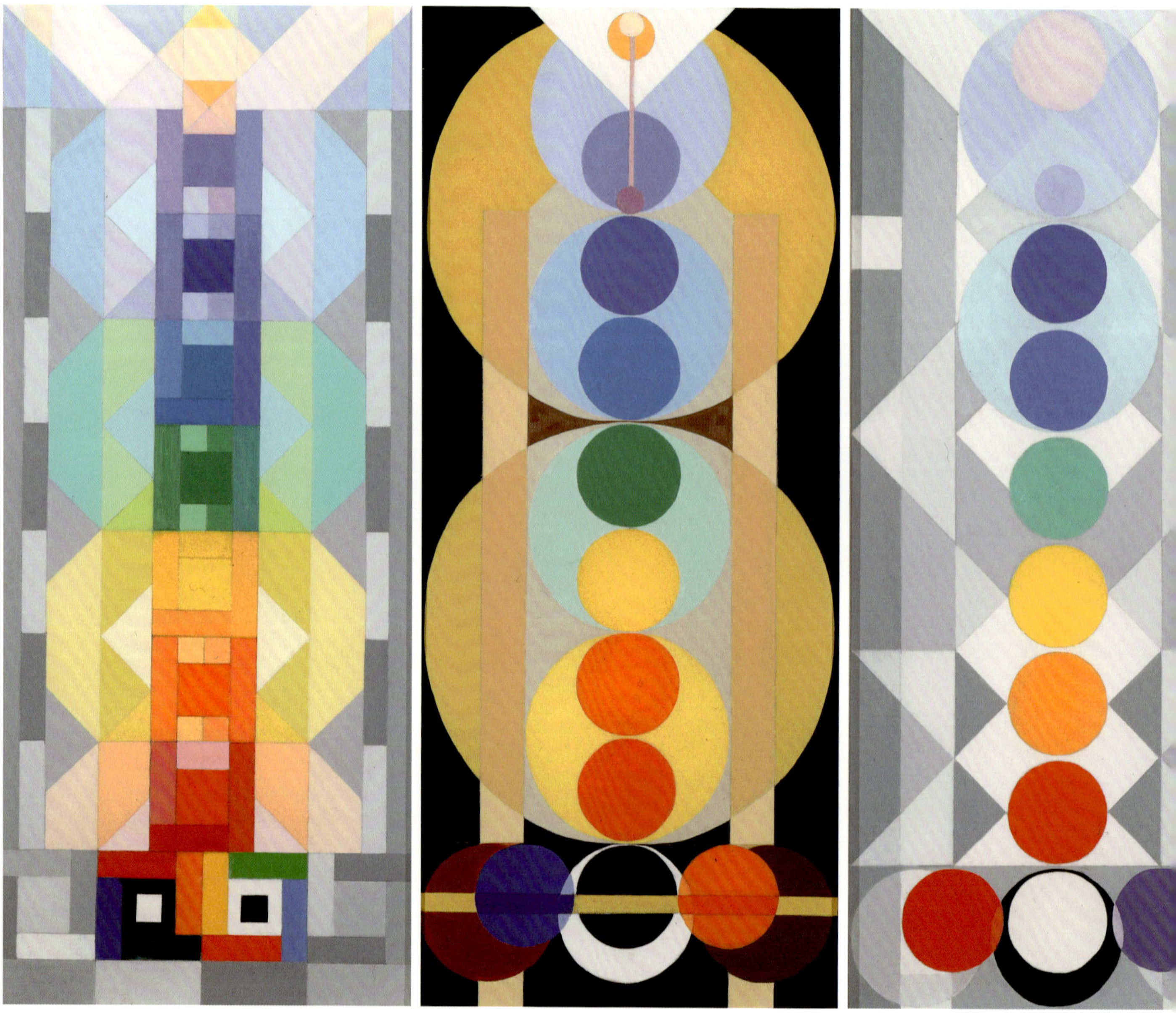

6

CHARMION VON WIEGAND

Triptych, Number 700, 1961

Oil on canvas

Three panels, overall: 42 ¼ × 54 in. (107.3 × 137.2 cm)

Three panels, each: 42 ¼ × 18 in. (107.3 × 45.7 cm)

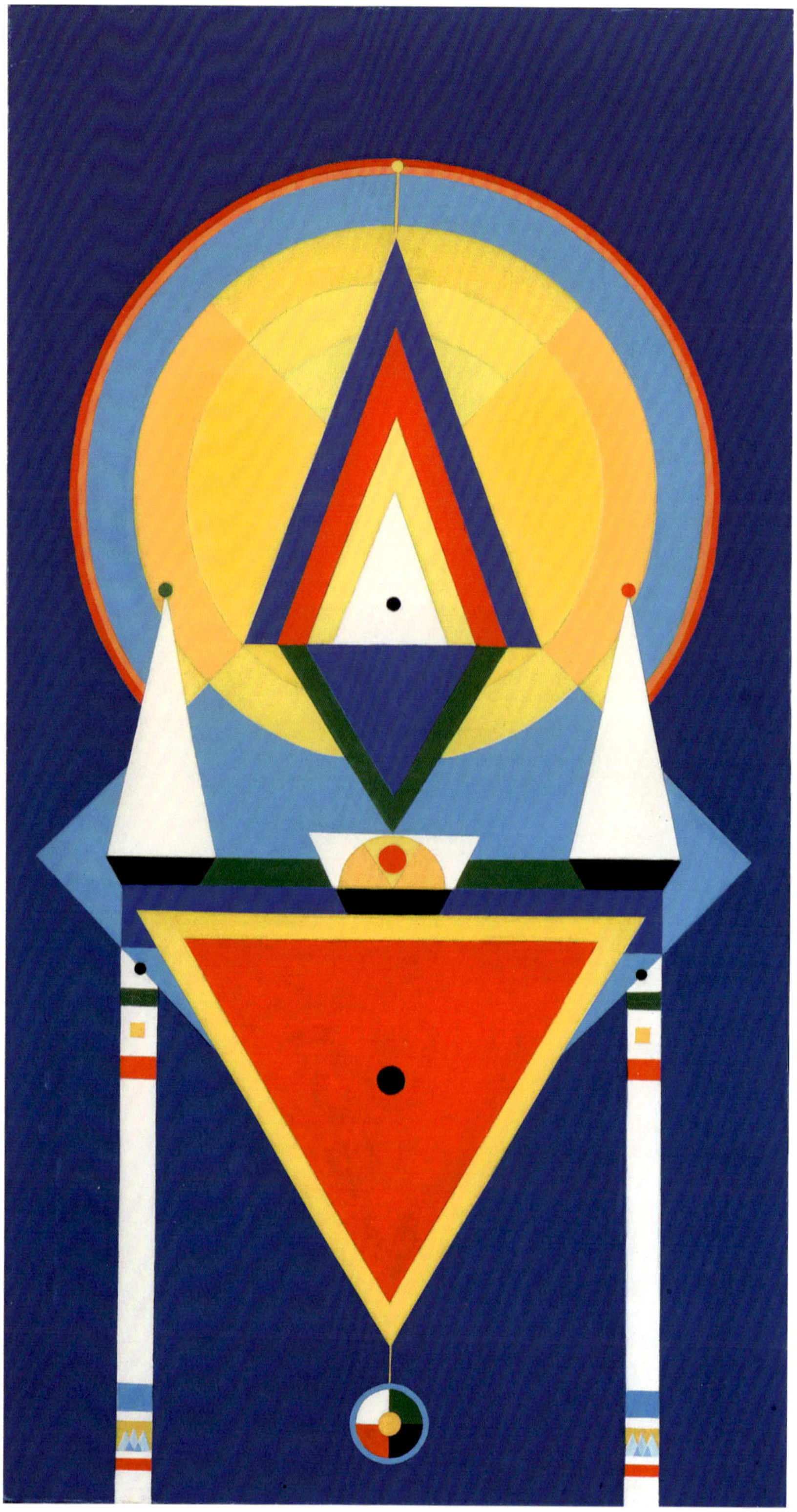

7

CHARMION VON WIEGAND

"Nothing that is wrong in principle can be right in practice."—Carl Schurz, 1829–1906.

From the series Great Ideas of Western Man, 1966

Oil and pencil on canvas

49 7/8 × 27 1/8 in. (128.8 × 68.8 cm)

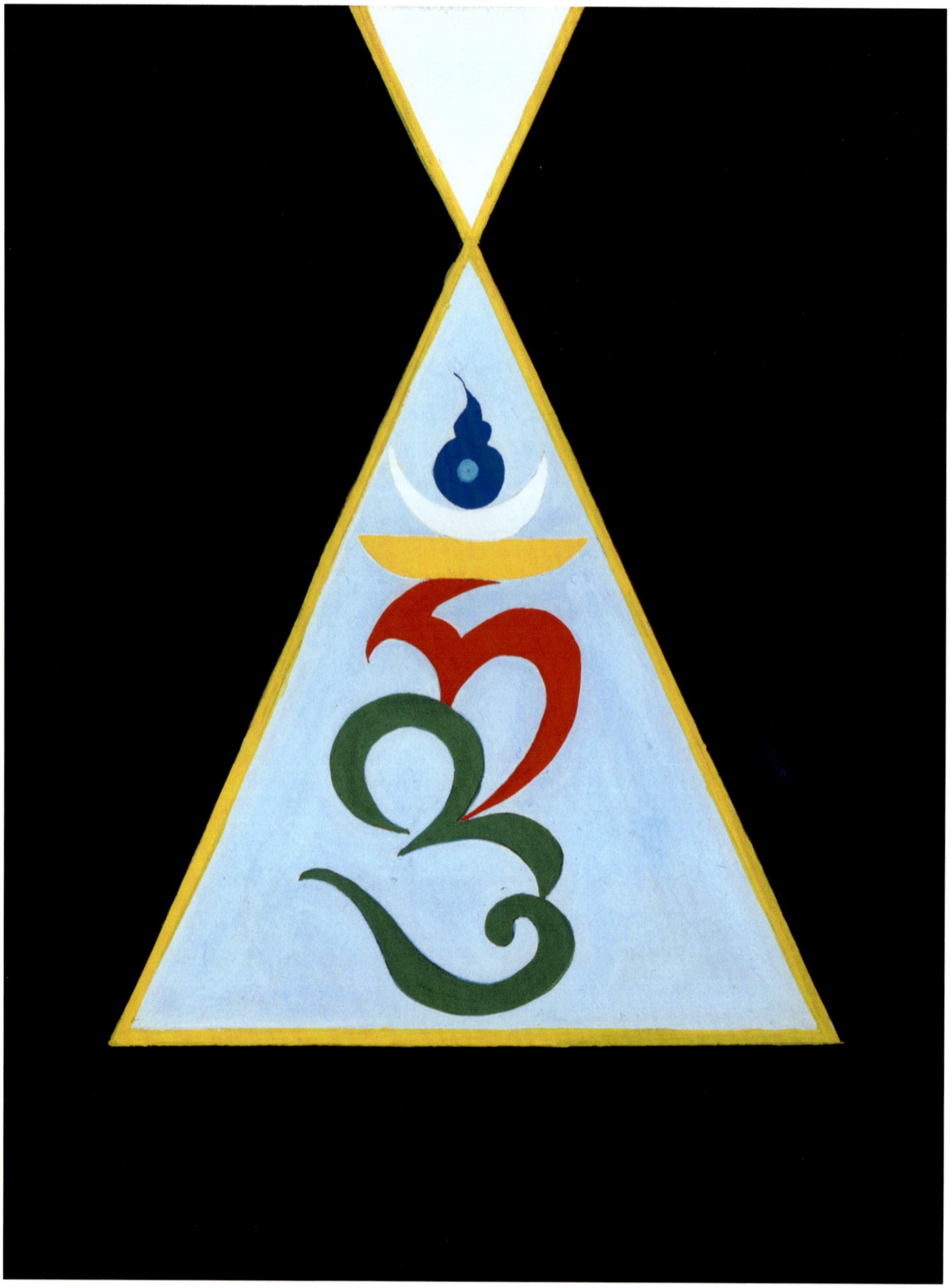

8

CHARMION VON WIEGAND

Gouache #163: The Letter Hum, 1962

Gouache on paperboard

16 ½ × 12 × ½ in. (41.9 × 30.6 × 1.3 cm), signed

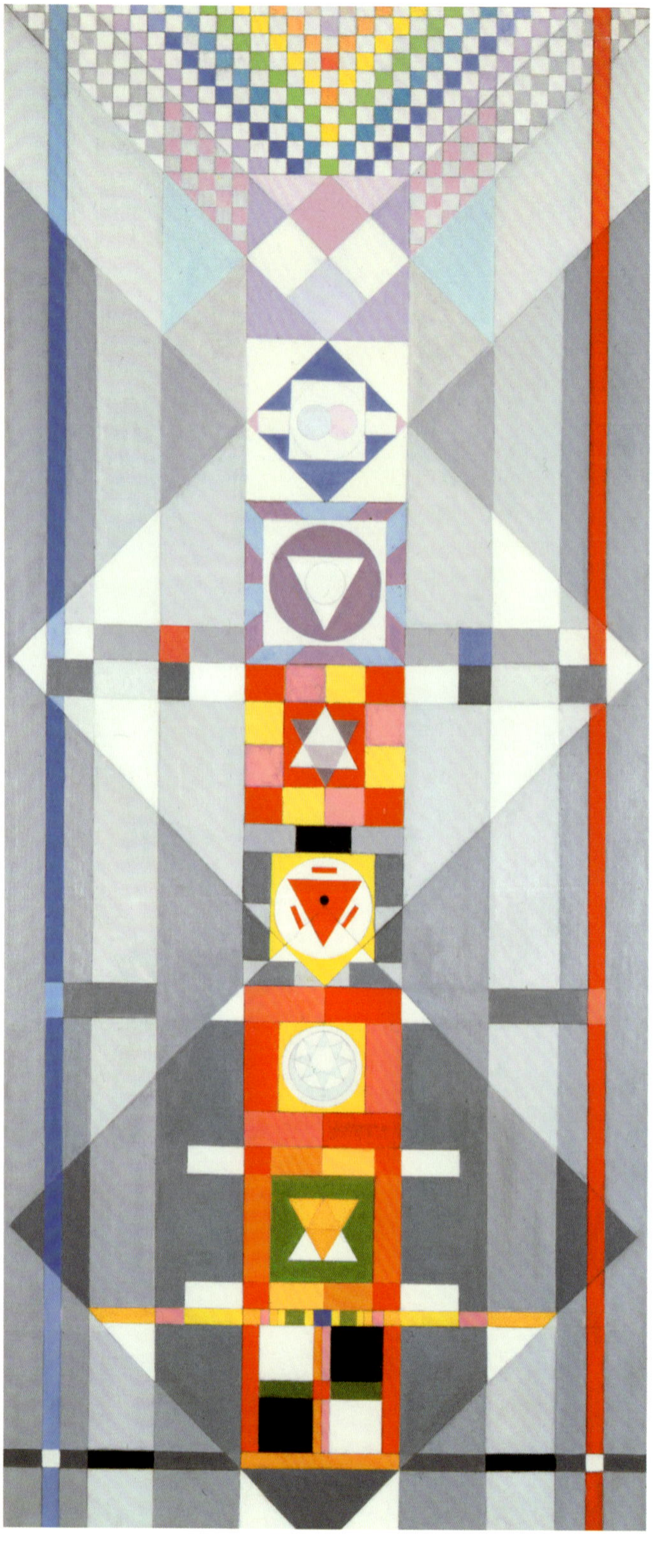

9

CHARMION VON WIEGAND

The Chakras, 1958–68

Oil on canvas

64 × 28 in. (162.6 × 71.1 cm), signed and dated

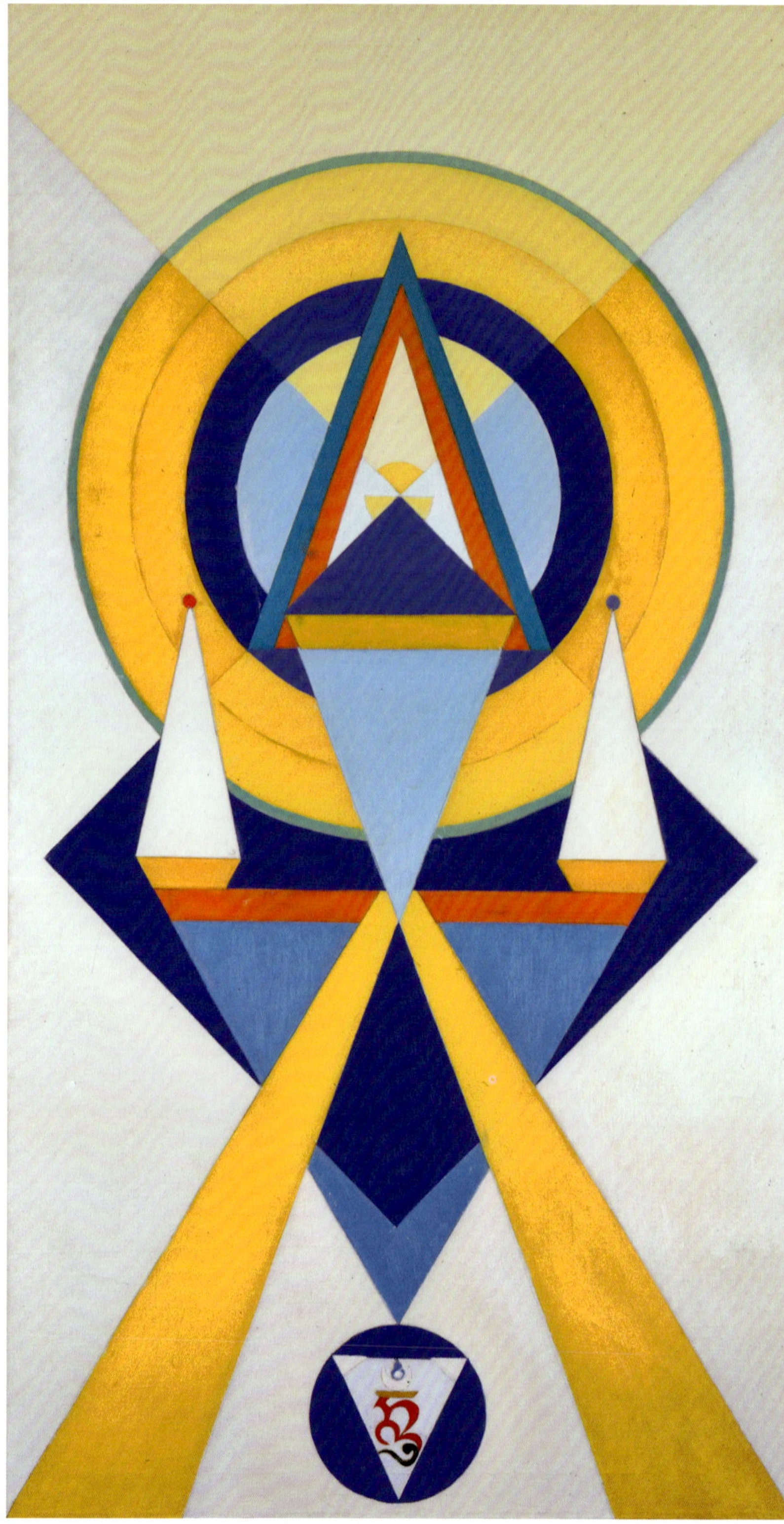

10

CHARMION VON WIEGAND

To the Adi Buddha, ca. 1968–1970

Oil on canvas

50 × 27 in. (127 × 68.6 cm), signed

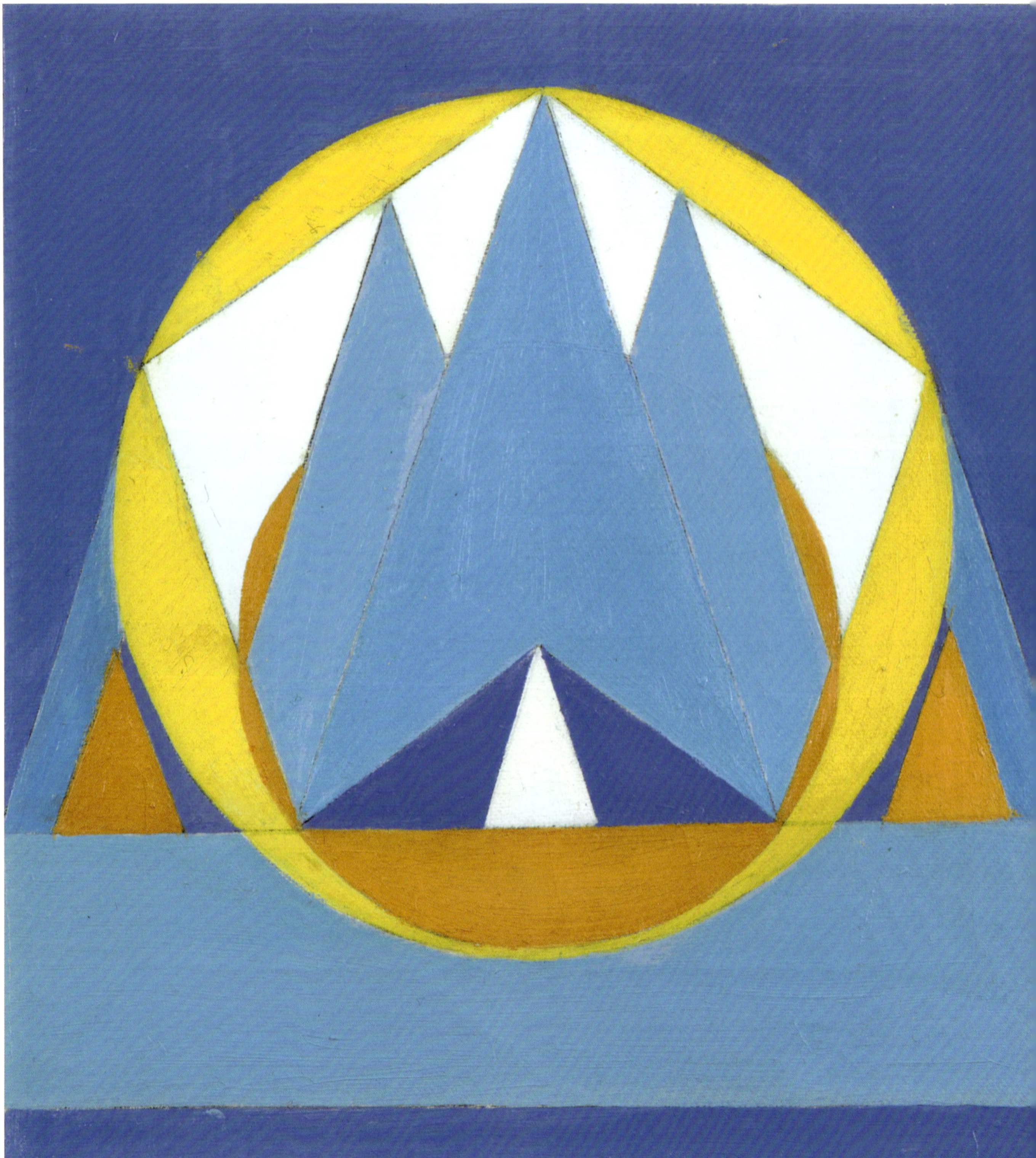

11

CHARMION VON WIEGAND

Untitled, 1951

Oil on canvas

10 × 10 in. (25.4 × 25.4 cm), signed

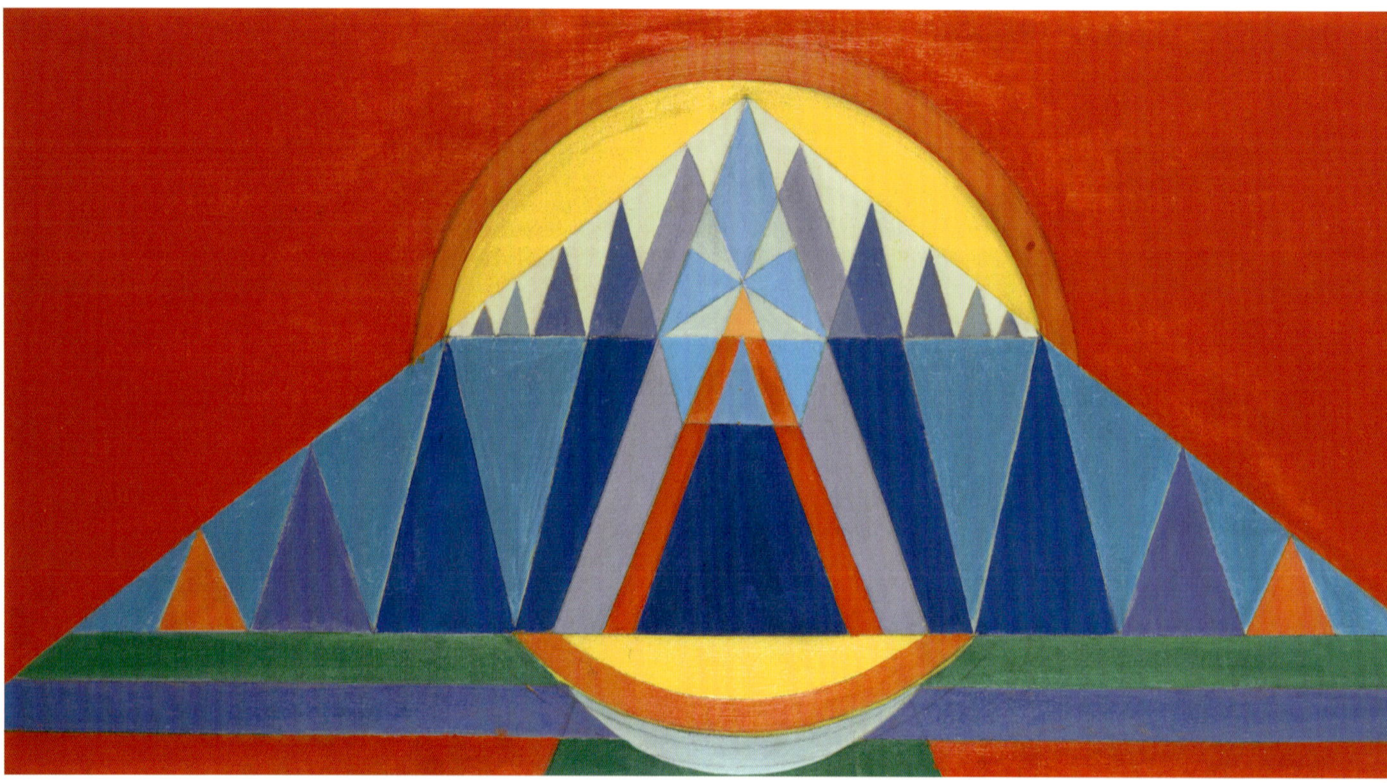

12

CHARMION VON WIEGAND
Untitled, 1964
Oil on masonite
14 × 28 in. (35.6 × 71.1 cm), signed

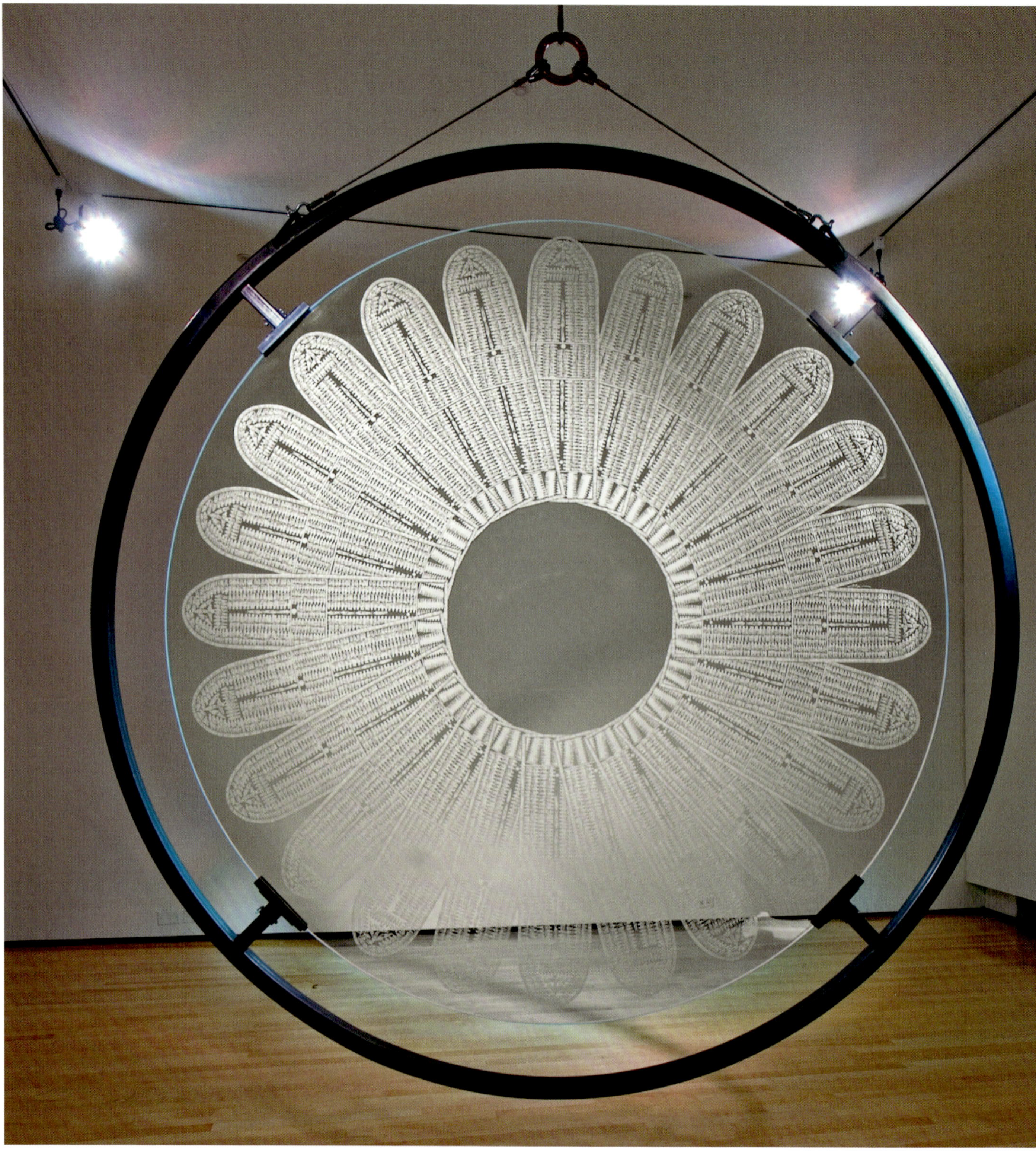

13

SANFORD BIGGERS
Lotus, 2007
Hand-etched glass, steel, LED's
Diameter: 7 ft. (213.4 cm)
Installation at Grand Arts, 2007

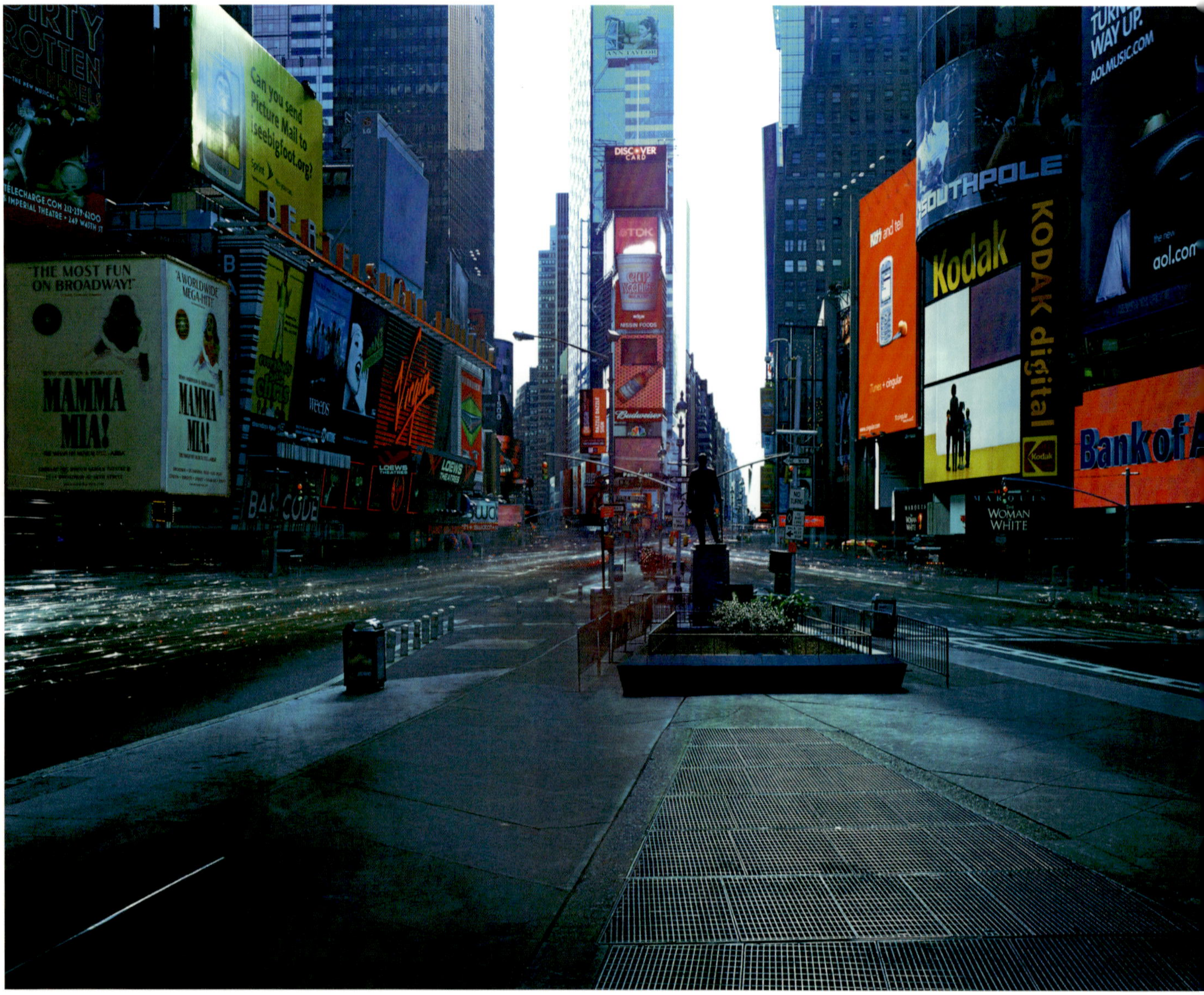

"THE MOST FUN ON BROADWAY!"
MAMMA MIA!
"A WORLDWIDE MEGA-HIT"
MAMMA MIA!
Can you send Picture Mail to iseebigfoot.org?
DISCOVER CARD
TDK
NISSIN FOODS
Budweiser
Virgin
LOEWS THEATRES
AOLMUSIC.COM
SOUTHPOLE
Kodak
KODAK digital
WOMAN WHITE

14

ATTA KIM

ON-AIR Project 110–2, The New York Series, Times Square, 2005

Chromogenic print

65⅜ × 49⅝ in. (166 × 126 cm)

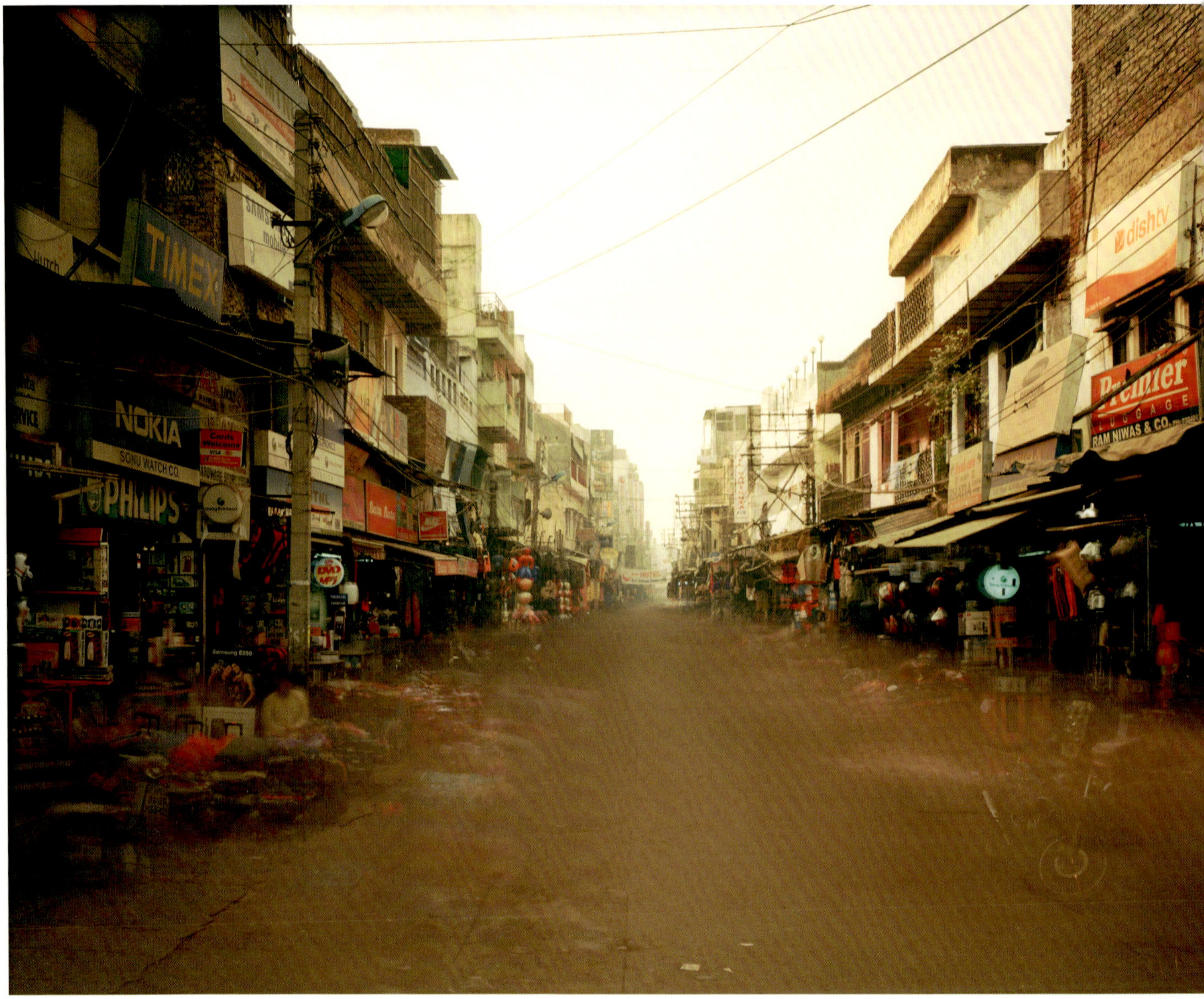
TIMEX
NOKIA
SONU WATCH CO.
PHILIPS
dishtv
LUGGAGE
RAM NIWAS & CO.

15

ATTA KIM

ON-AIR Project 160–13, The India Series, Paharganj in New Delhi, 2007

Chromogenic print

65⅜ × 49⅝ in. (166 × 126 cm)

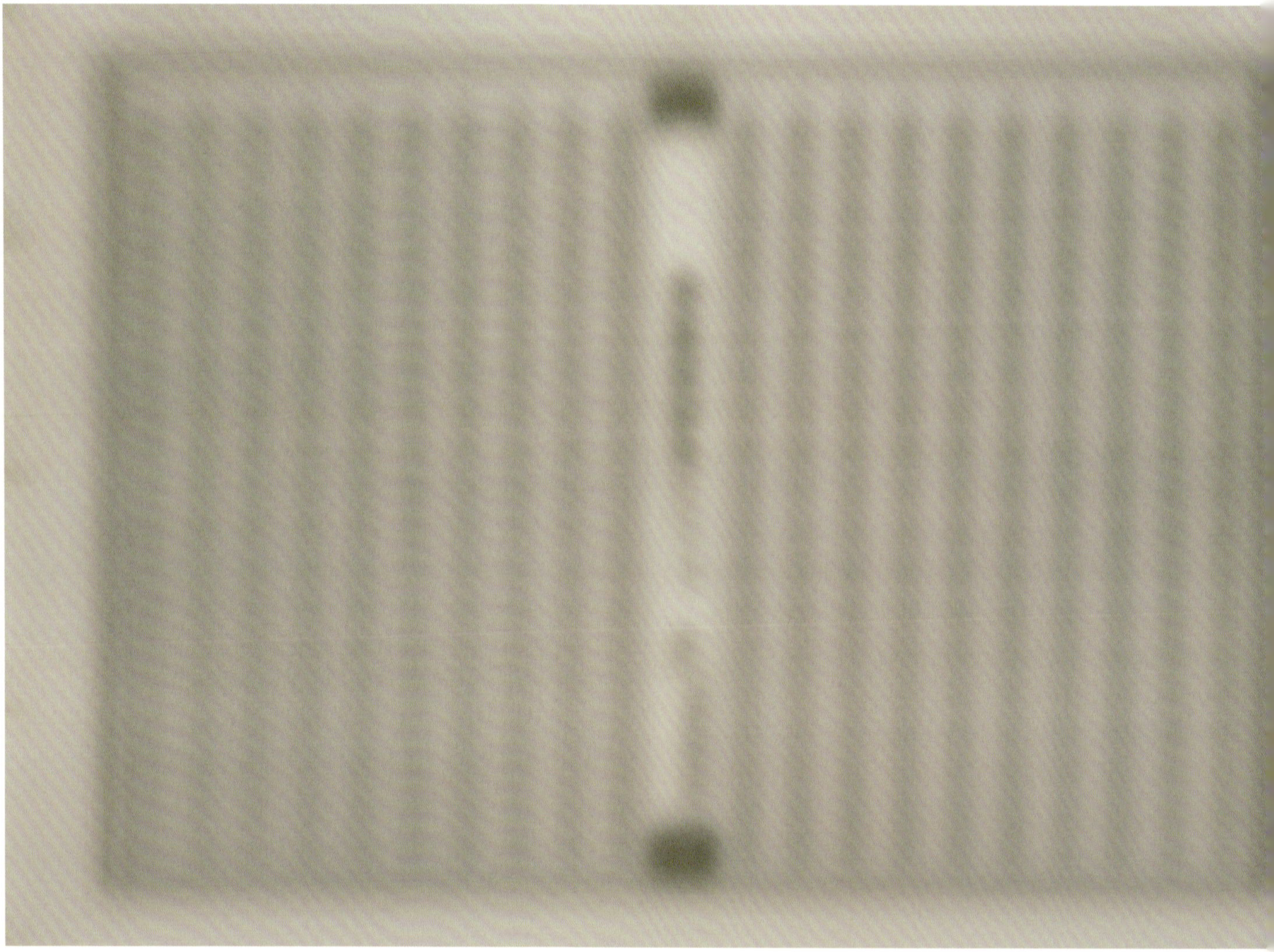

16

ATTA KIM

ON-AIR Project 5844, The Avatamsaka Sutra, 2007

Chromogenic print

35⅜ × 51½ in. (89.9 × 13.8 cm)

17

ATTA KIM
ON-AIR Project, New York–10,000, 2008
Chromogenic print
92 ½ × 71 in. (235 × 180 cm)

18

ATTA KIM

ON-AIR Project, William Turner, 2009

Chromogenic print

97 5/8 × 71 in. (248 × 180 cm)

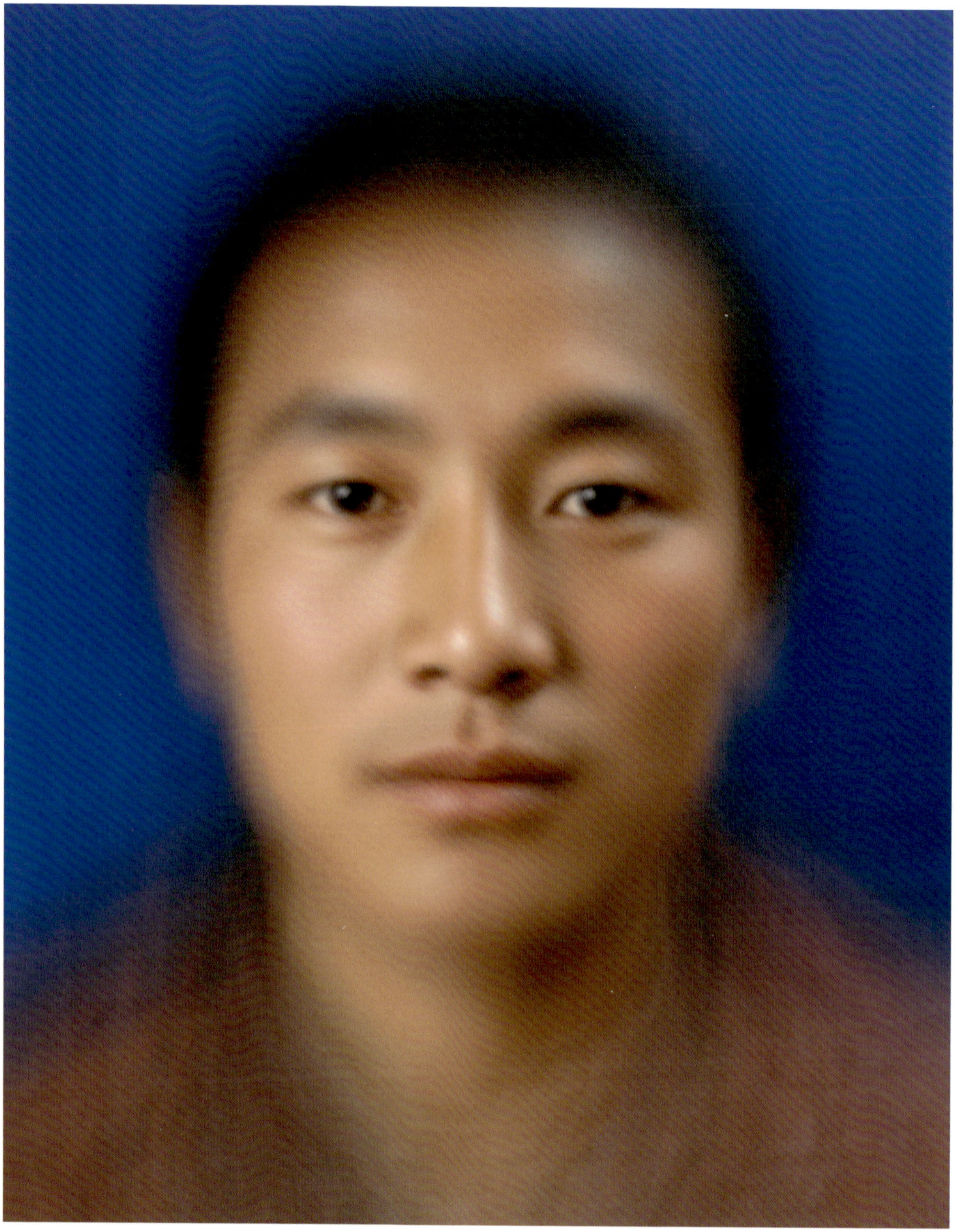

19

ATTA KIM

ON-AIR Project 104–1, The Self-Portrait Series, 100 Men (*Tibetan*), 2005

Chromogenic print

52¾ × 65⅜ in. (166 × 134 cm)

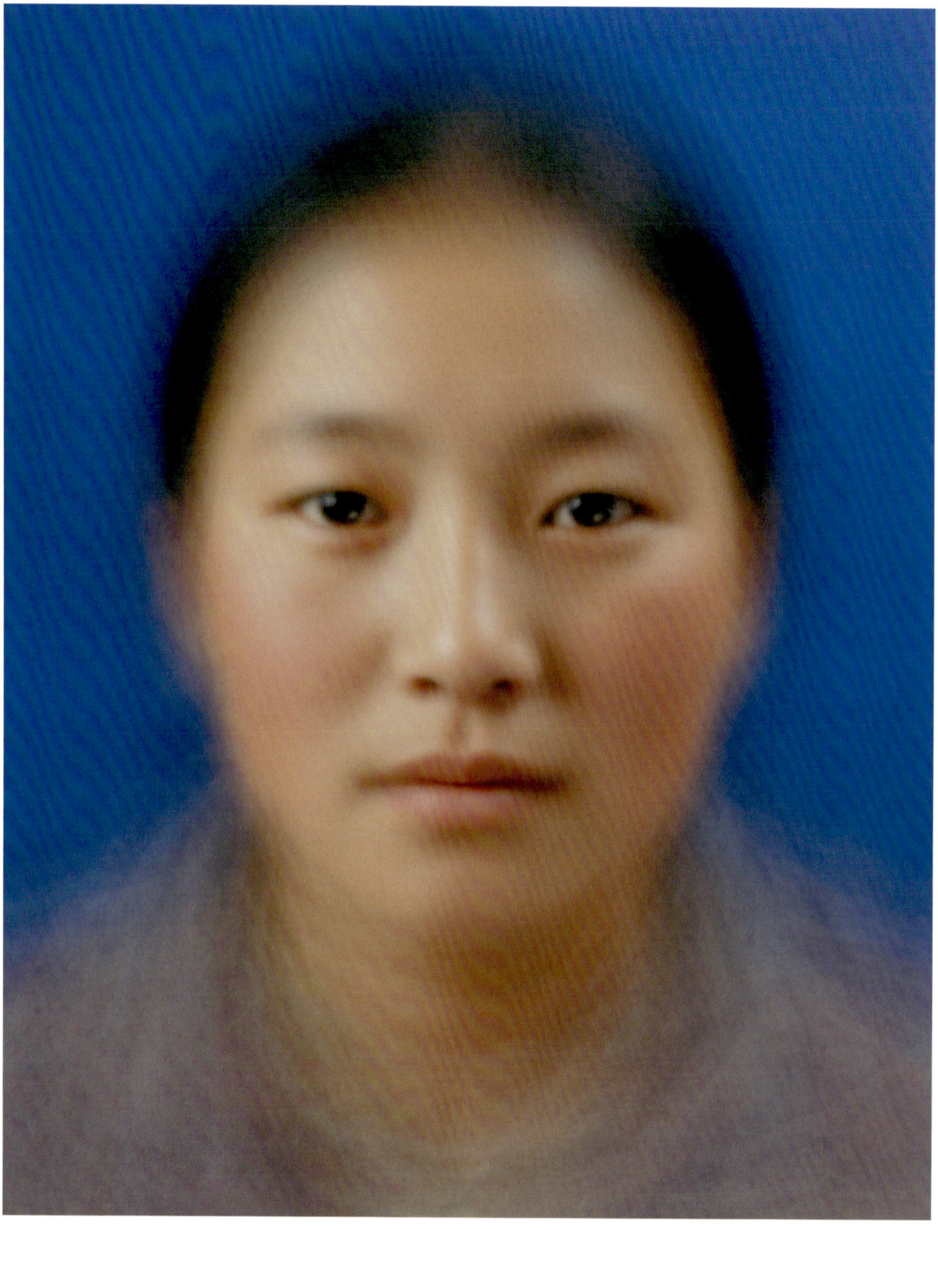

20

ATTA KIM

ON-AIR Project 105–1, The Self-Portrait Series, 100 Women (*Tibetan*), 2005

Chromogenic print

52¾ × 65⅜ in. (166 × 134 cm)

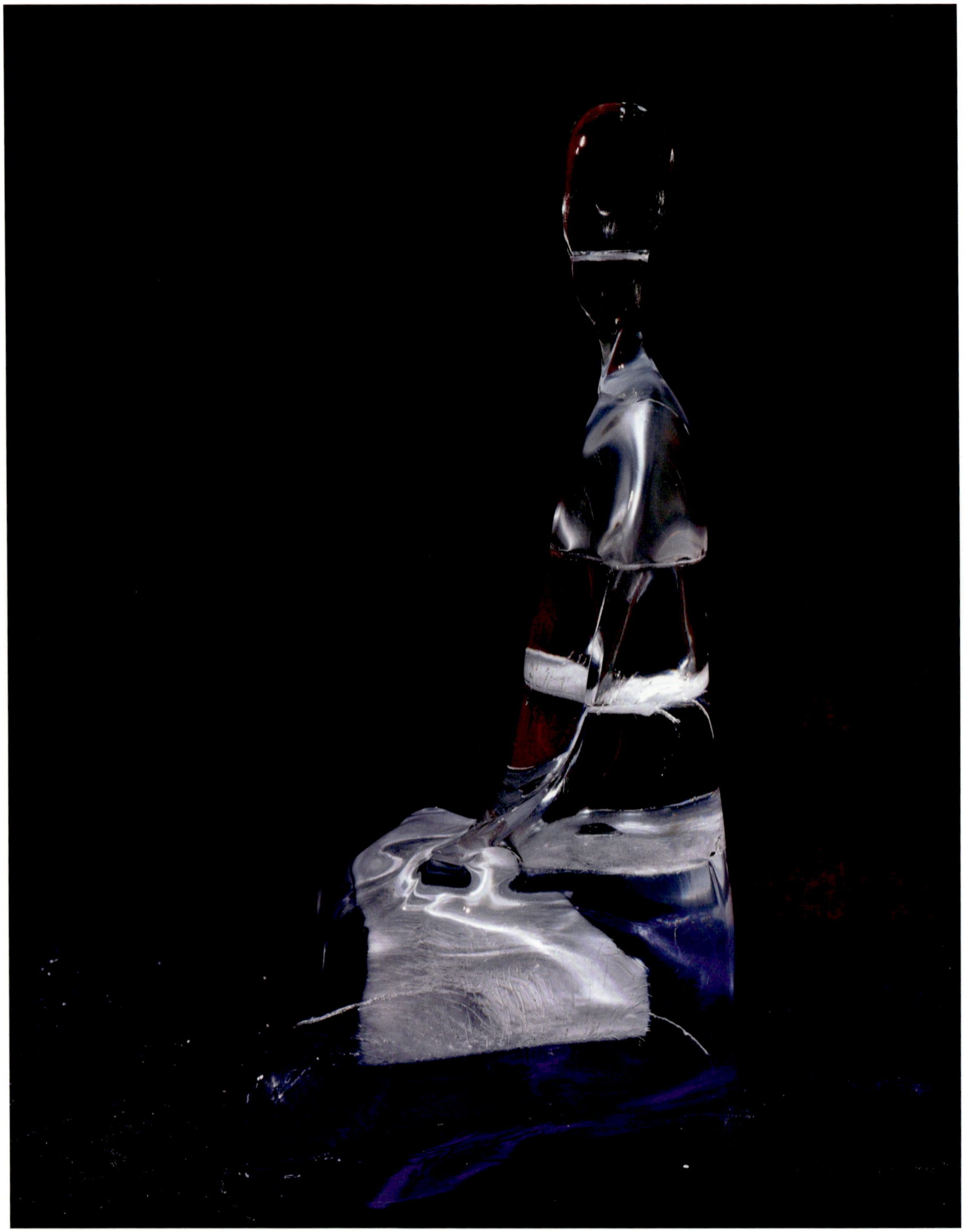

21

ATTA KIM

ON-AIR Project 141–3, The Monologue of Ice Series, Buddha, 2006

Chromogenic print

52¾ × 65⅜ in. (166 × 134 cm)

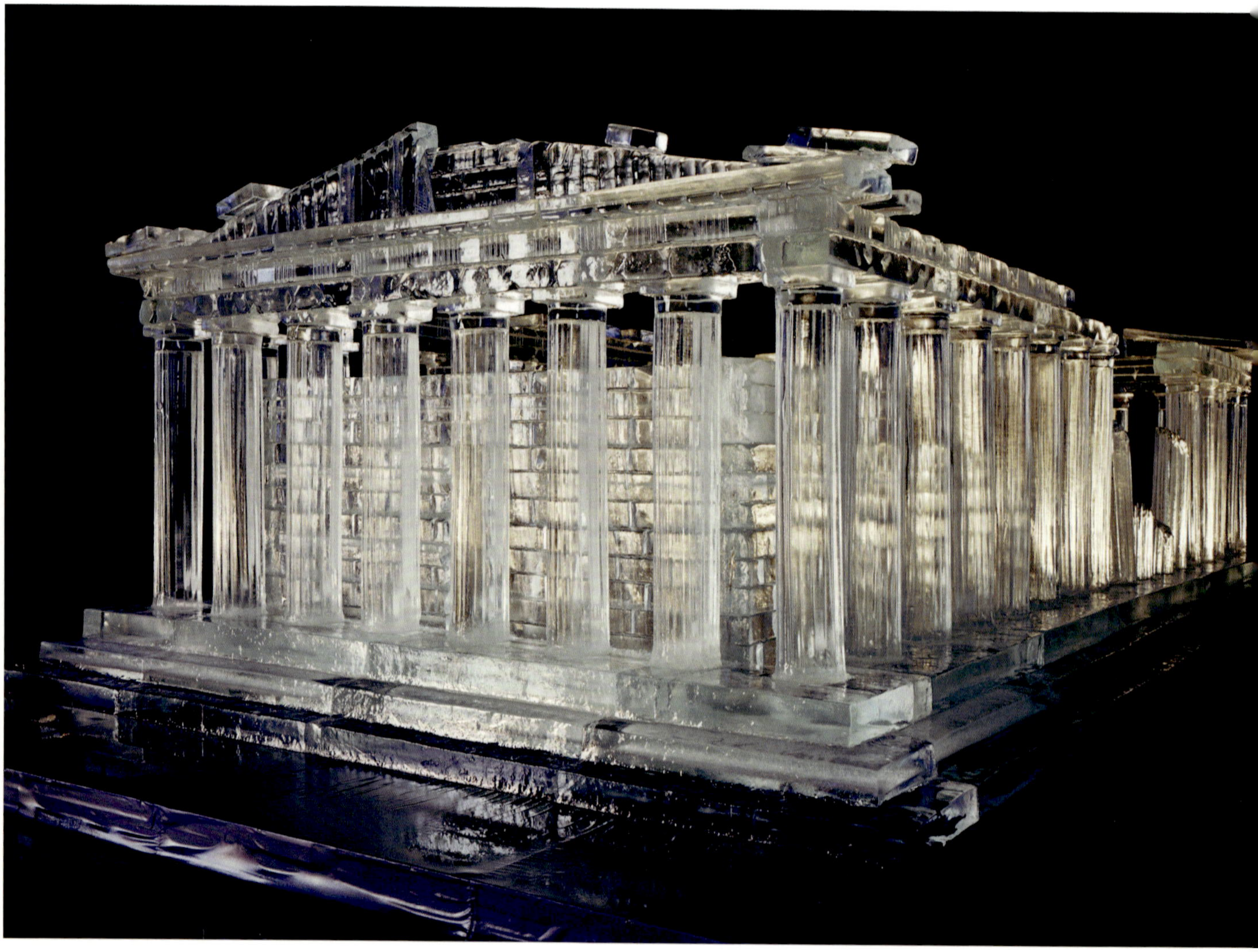

22

ATTA KIM

ON-AIR Project, The Monologue of Ice Series, Parthenon, 2008

Video

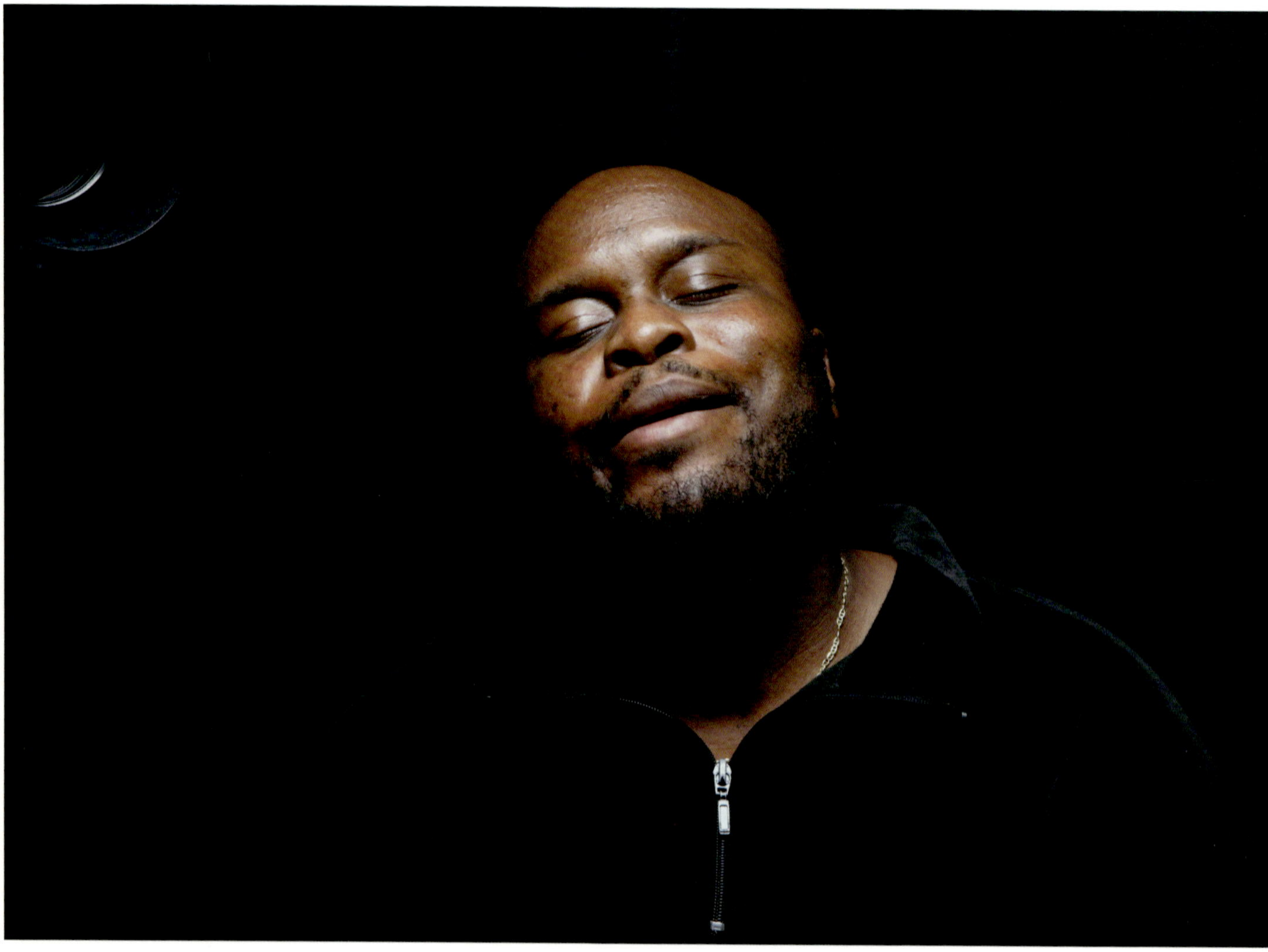

23

THEASTER GATES
Breathing, 2010
Video installation
Performers: Khari Lemuel, Yaw Agyeman,
Charisma Sweat, Aya-Nicole Cook, and Daya Lynn

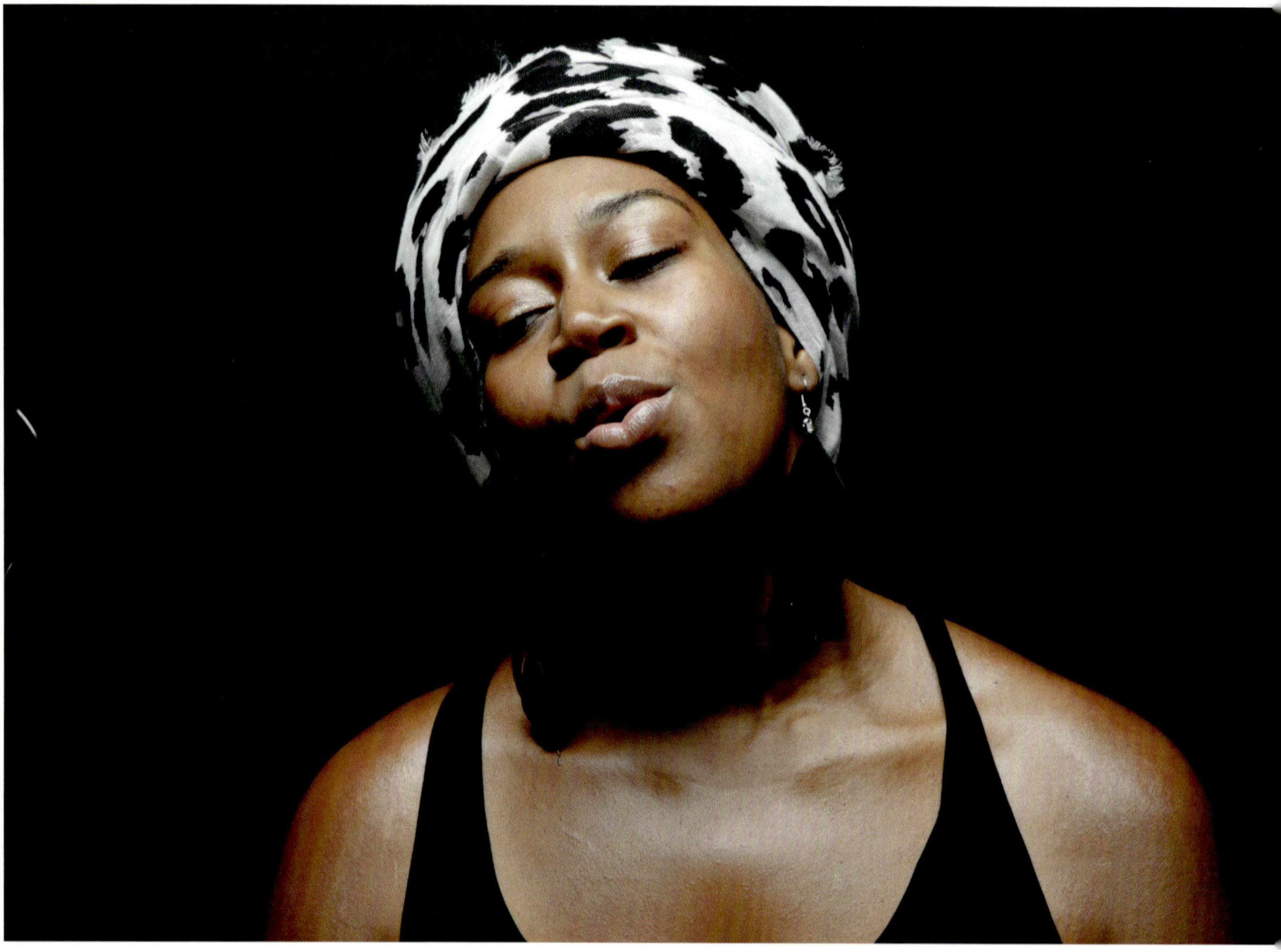

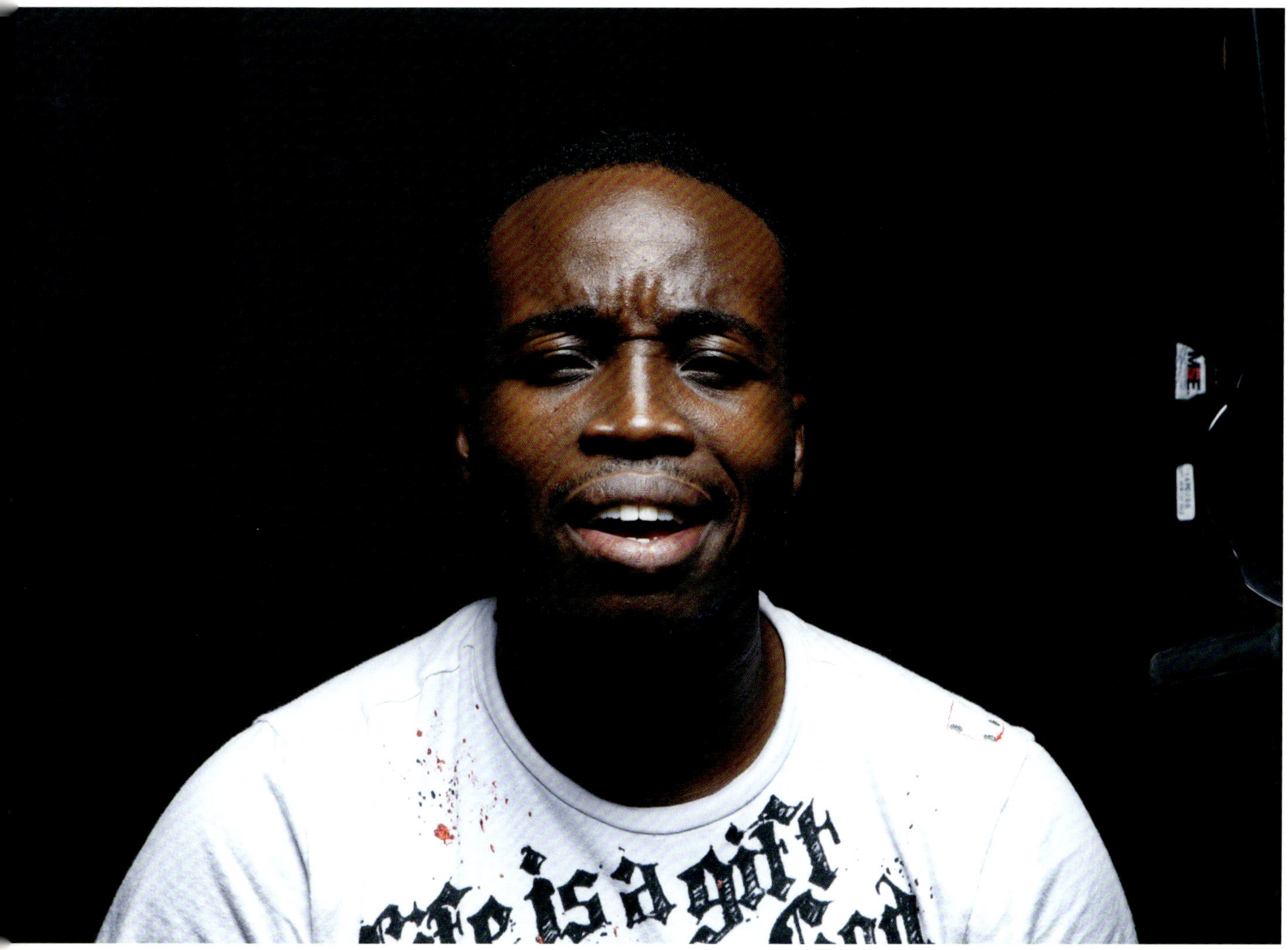

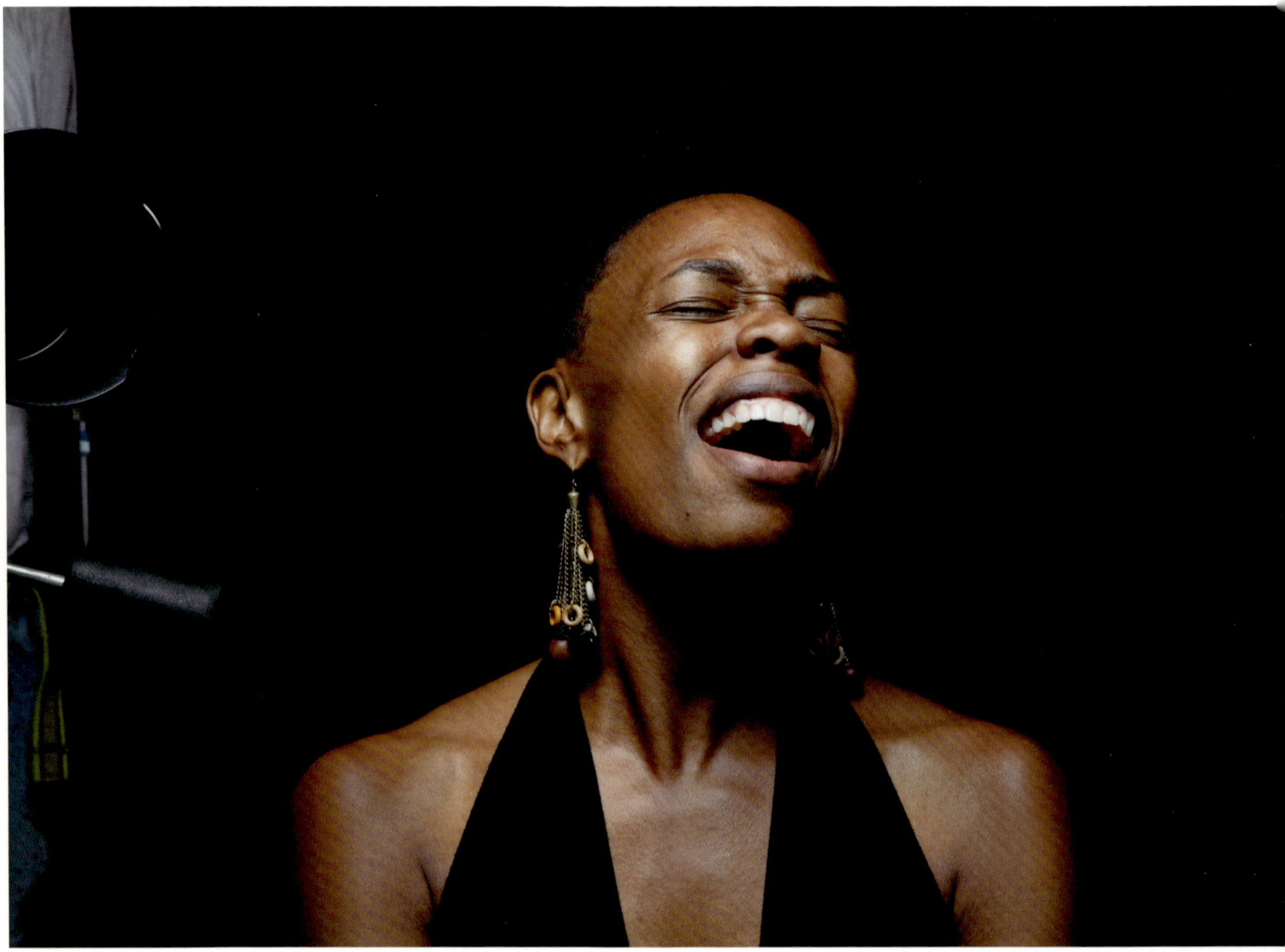

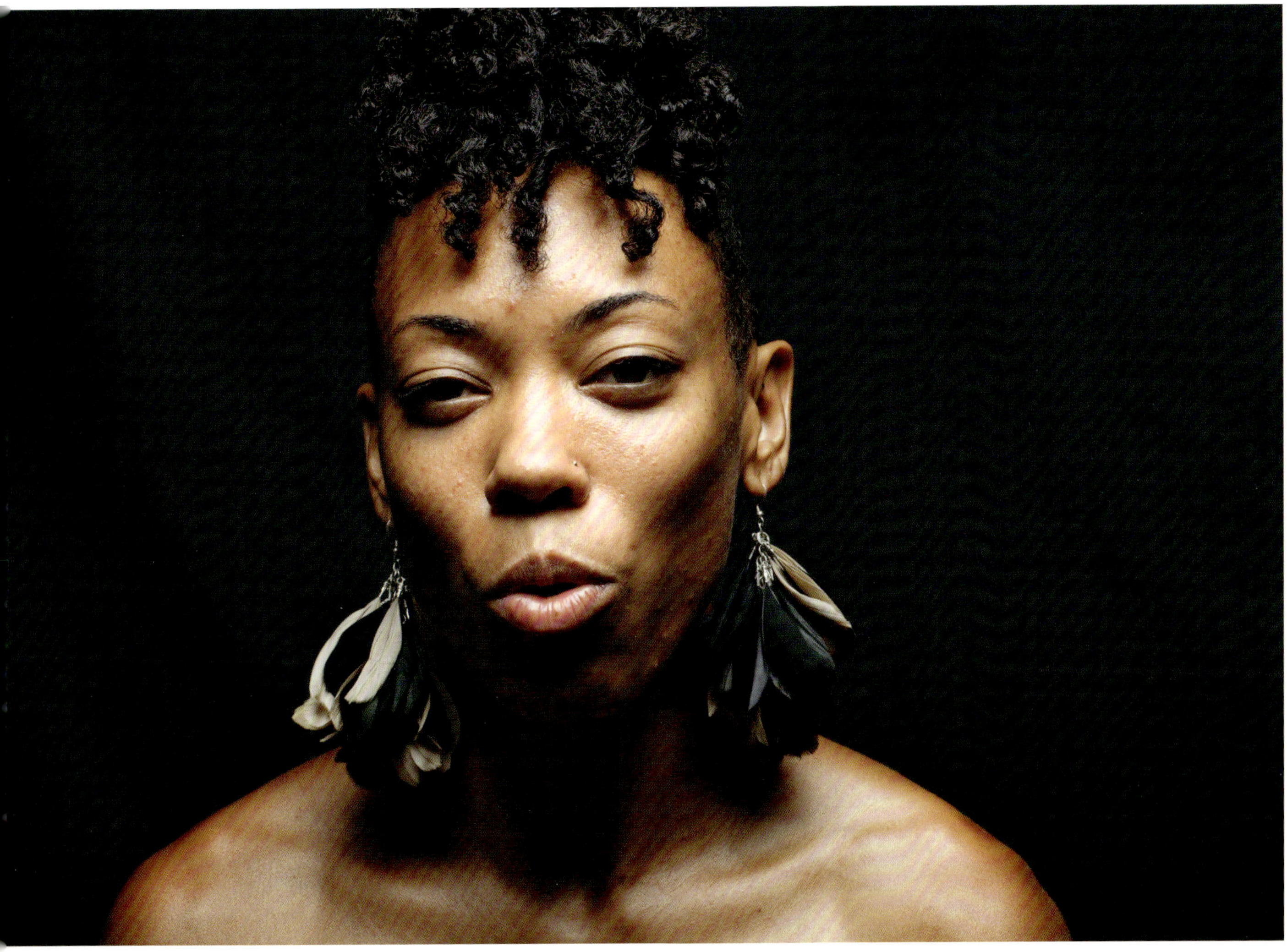

WORKS IN THE EXHIBITIION

PLATE 1
Wolfgang Laib. *Rice Meals,* 2010. 33 brass plates, rice, and hazelnut pollen. Approximate length: 53 ft. 4 in. (16.26 m). © Wolfgang Laib. Courtesy of the artist and Sean Kelly Gallery, New York.

PLATE 2
Wolfgang Laib. *Milkstone,* 2010. White marble, milk. 2⅜ × 20½ × 24½ in. (6 × 52 × 62 cm). © Wolfgang Laib. Courtesy of the artist and Sean Kelly Gallery, New York.

PLATE 3
Wolfgang Laib. *Untitled* (*Stairs*), 2002. Burmese red lacquer and wood. 126 × 29⅛ × 72⅜ in. (320 × 74 × 184 cm). Private Collection, Stuttgart. © Wolfgang Laib. Courtesy of the artist and Sean Kelly Gallery, New York.

PLATE 4
Wolfgang Laib. *Rice House,* 2009. Marble and rice. 8¼ × 4¾ × 39 in. (21 × 12 × 99 cm). © Wolfgang Laib. Courtesy of the artist and Sean Kelly Gallery, New York

PLATE 5
Charmion von Wiegand. *The Ascent to Mt. Meru,* 1962. Gouache on paper. 23⅜ × 18⅜ in. (59.4 × 46.7 cm). Solomon R. Guggenheim Museum, New York. Gift, Ruth Abrams in memory of Gerald Scofield, 1982. 82.2931. Courtesy of Michael Rosenfeld Gallery, LLC, New York.

PLATE 6
Charmion von Wiegand. *Triptych, Number 700,* 1961. Oil on canvas. Three panels, overall: 42¼ × 54 in. (107.3 × 137.2 cm); each: 42¼ × 18 in. (107.3 × 45.7 cm). Whitney Museum of American Art, New York. Gift of Alvin M. Greenstein, 62.39. Photography by Geoffrey Clements. Courtesy of Michael Rosenfeld Gallery, LLC, New York.

PLATE 7
Charmion von Wiegand. *"Nothing that is wrong in principle can be right in practice."—Carl Schurz, 1829–1906. From the series Great Ideas of Western Man*, 1966. Oil and pencil on canvas. 49⅞ × 27⅛ in. (128.8 × 68.8 cm). Smithsonian American Art Museum, Gift of Container Corporation of America. 1984.124.300. Courtesy of Michael Rosenfeld Gallery, LLC, New York.

PLATE 8
Charmion von Wiegand. *Gouache #163: The Letter Hum,* 1962. Gouache on paperboard. 16½ × 12 × ½ in. (41.9 × 30.6 × 1.3 cm), signed. Courtesy of Michael Rosenfeld Gallery, LLC, New York.

PLATE 9
Charmion von Wiegand. *The Chakras,* 1958–68. Oil on canvas. 64 × 28 in. (162.6 × 71.1 cm), signed and dated. Collection of Hank and Carol Brown Goldberg. Courtesy of Michael Rosenfeld Gallery, LLC, New York.

PLATE 10
Charmion von Wiegand. *To the Adi Buddha*, ca. 1968–1970. Oil on canvas. 50 × 27 in. (127 × 68.6 cm), signed. Courtesy of Michael Rosenfeld Gallery, LLC, New York.

PLATE 11
Charmion von Wiegand. *Untitled*, 1951. Oil on canvas. 10 × 10 in. (25.4 × 25.4 cm), signed. Courtesy of Michael Rosenfeld Gallery, LLC, New York.

PLATE 12
Charmion von Wiegand. *Untitled*, 1964. Oil on masonite. 14 × 28 in. (35.6 × 71.1 cm), signed. Courtesy of Michael Rosenfeld Gallery, LLC, New York.

PLATE 13
Sanford Biggers. *Lotus*, 2007. Hand-etched glass, steel, LED's. Diameter: 7 ft. (213.4 cm). Installation at Grand Arts, 2007. Courtesy of the artist.

PLATE 14
Atta Kim. *ON-AIR Project 110–2, The New York Series, Times Square*, 2005. Chromogenic print. 65⅜ × 49⅝ in. (166 × 126 cm). Courtesy of the artist.

PLATE 15
Atta Kim. *ON-AIR Project 160–13, The India Series, Paharganj in New Delhi*, 2007. Chromogenic print. 65⅜ × 49⅝ in. (166 × 126 cm). Courtesy of the artist.

PLATE 16
Atta Kim. *ON-AIR Project 5844, The Avatamsaka Sutra*, 2007. Chromogenic print. 35⅜ × 51½ in. (89.9 × 130.8 cm). Courtesy of the artist.

PLATE 17
Atta Kim. *ON-AIR Project, New York–10,000*, 2008. Chromogenic print. 92½ × 71 in. (235 × 180 cm). Courtesy of the artist.

PLATE 18
Atta Kim. *ON-AIR Project, William Turner*, 2009. Chromogenic print. 97⅝ × 71 in. (248 × 180 cm). Courtesy of the artist.

PLATE 19
Atta Kim. *ON-AIR Project 104–1, The Self-Portrait Series, 100 Men* (*Tibetan*), 2005. Chromogenic print. 52¾ × 65⅜ in. (166 × 134 cm). Courtesy of the artist.

PLATE 20
Atta Kim. *ON-AIR Project 105–1, The Self-Portrait Series, 100 Women* (*Tibetan*), 2005. Chromogenic print. 52¾ × 65⅜ in. (166 × 134 cm). Courtesy of the artist.

PLATE 21
Atta Kim. *ON-AIR Project 141–3, The Monologue of Ice Series, Buddha*, 2006. Chromogenic print. 52¾ × 65⅜ in. (166 × 134 cm). Courtesy of the artist.

PLATE 22
Atta Kim. *ON-AIR Project, The Monologue of Ice Series, Parthenon*, 2008. Video. Courtesy of the artist.

PLATE 23
Theaster Gates. *Breathing*, 2010. Video installation. Performers: Khari Lemuel, Yaw Agyeman, Charisma Sweat, Aya-Nicole Cook, and Daya Lynn. Courtesy of the artist.

ARTIST BIOGRAPHIES

Born in South Korea in 1956, **ATTA KIM** graduated from Changwon University with a degree in mechanical engineering and has been actively creating and displaying photography since the mid-1980s. In elaborate projects ranging from Buddhas formed from ice to re-imagined photographs of the *Mona Lisa*, Kim counters the political with the imaginary, the traditional with the subversive. He has used extended exposures to vanish people from crowded cities, photographed nude models in desolate landscapes and museum galleries, and overlaid photographs to create people and images both familiar and unearthly. Kim has held solo shows at the Samsung Photo Gallery, Seoul; the Nikon Salon Gallery, Tokyo; the Yechong Gallery, Seoul; and has been included in numerous group exhibitions, including shows at the Museum of Contemporary Photography in Chicago; The Odense Foto Triennale in Odense, Denmark; the Australian Centre for Photography; the twenty-fifth São Paulo Biennial; and FotoFest in Houston. Kim lives and works in Seoul and New York City.

WOLFGANG LAIB (b. 1950) works in the infinitesimal, using natural materials to form subtle installations steadily building upon each other without one piece ever overshadowing another. After obtaining a doctorate in medicine at the University of Tübingen, Laib felt dissatisfied with only healing the body. He turned to art, believing in its healing for all humanity, and created his first milkstone in 1975. Flower pollen works began in 1977, followed by rice in 1983, and beeswax in 1987. Each piece reflects upon the ephemeral aspects of life in its beauty and incredible delicacy. Laib's work has been shown at the Hirshhorn Museum and Sculpture Garden, Washington, DC; the Fondation Beyeler, Basel, Switzerland; Art Gallery of New South Wales, Sydney, Australia; The National Museum of Modern Art, Tokyo; and Sperone Westwater, New York. Laib lives in Germany.

The American abstract artist **CHARMION VON WIEGAND** (1896–1983) drew much of her inspiration from Tibetan Buddhism and Mahayana. Born in Chicago and raised in Arizona, San Francisco, and Berlin, von Wiegand attended Columbia University until she left to become a playwright. She traveled to Moscow in 1929 as a journalist, work that brought her back to New York City and introduced her to Piet Mondrian in 1941. The two became great friends, and admiration for Mondrian's work led von Wiegand to her own abstract paintings. At first inspired by Mondrian's neo-plasticism, she became fascinated by Buddhist mysticism, and her work is now celebrated for its abstract expressions of complex religious ideas. She was president of the American Abstract Artists from 1951 to 1953 and was elected to the American Academy of Arts and Letters in 1980. The Bass Museum of Art in Miami Beach, Florida, organized her first retrospective in 1982. Von Wiegand's work has been shown at the Solomon R. Guggenheim Museum, the Hirshhorn Museum and Sculpture Garden, The Metropolitan Museum of Art, the Museum of Modern Art, and the Whitney Museum of American Art.

SANFORD BIGGERS, a New York resident born in Los Angeles in 1970, combines ideas and cultures as he combines performance and installation. Known for combining hip-hop culture and black experiences with Buddhism in the forms of sand painting and religious proverb performance, Biggers incorporates spirituality and urban culture to demonstrate the interconnection of all people. Biggers has held exhibitions at the Solomon R. Guggenheim Museum in New York; The Project, New York; and Triple Candie Gallery, New York. Other works by Biggers have been on display at Tate Britain and Tate Modern, London; Whitney Museum of American Art; the Studio Museum in Harlem; and the Yerba Buena Center for the Arts, San Francisco; as well as institutions in China, Germany, Hungary, Japan, Poland, and Russia. Biggers is currently a full-time faculty at the Virginia Commonwealth University Sculpture and Expanded Media Program.

Chicagoan **THEASTER GATES** (b. 1973) is an urban planner, potter, educator, and artist. A graduate of Iowa State University and University of Cape Town, Gates draws on local traditions and societal norms to address political and social questions, using performance, music, and urban development to connect disparate people and cultures. Through subtle class differences between a shoe shiner and a customer, or in cultural hybrids of Japanese and African American dinner parties, Gates composes art events that bring people together. Gates is a 2010 Whitney Biennial Finalist and is Coordinator of Art Programming at the University of Chicago. His work has been shown at the Milwaukee Art Museum, Chicago Cultural Center, Iowa State University, and St. George Cathedral, Cape Town, South Africa.

SELECTED BIBLIOGRAPHY

SANFORD BIGGERS

Baas, Jacquelynn, and Mary Jane Jacob. *Buddha Mind in Contemporary Art*. Berkeley: University of California Press. 2004.

Butter, Thomas. "Interview with Sanford Biggers." *Whitehot Magazine*, April 2010.

Cassel, Valerie. "Meditations of a B-Boy Buddhist: Sanford Biggers talks with Valerie Cassel Oliver." *The International Review of African American Art* (Vol. 2:3), 2007, 51–54.

"East Meets West: An Interview with Sanford Biggers." *Portland Art.net*, May 15, 2009.

Gaines, Malik. "Sanford Biggers: The Big Idea." *RVA Magazine* (Vol. 4:9), http://issuu.com/snook/docs/webrav_v4i9final/15.

Garcia, Miki. *Sanford Biggers: Moon Medicine.* Catalog by Santa Barbara Contemporary Arts Forum. March 3, 2010.

Performa 07, and RoseLee Goldberg. *Everywhere and all at once: an anthology of writings on Performa 07.* Zurich, Switzerland: JRP Ringier. 2009.

Rabinowitz, Cay-Sophie. "Blossom." *Grand Arts Exhibition Catalog,* October 2007.

Spaeth, Catherine. "A Walk Through 'Third Mind' at the Guggenheim with Sanford Biggers and Noah Fischer." Interview. *New York City Art Tours,* April 9, 2009.

Wilcox, Lauren. "Transformation and Tradition: Interview with Sanford Biggers." *Tout-Fait* (Duchamp Studies On-line Journal), 2001.

THEASTER GATES

Artist Connect Talk: Museum of the Art Institute. Interview. Podcast. November 3, 2007. http://www.artic.edu/aic/visitor_info/podcasts/artist_talks/Gates.html

Furnari, Rachel. "High Spirits: Artist Theaster Gates can't stop reaching new heights." *New City*, March 31, 2010 http://art.newcity.com/2010/03/30/.

Huang, Kelly. "An Artist and a Citizen." *Art 21 Blog*, October 30, 2009.

"Theaster Gates." 3Arts Foundation. Interview. Undated. http://www.3arts.org/pages/about-us/.

Turner, Lonnie. "Preview: Theaster Gates." *Art City*, April 13, 2010.

Viveros-Fauné, Christian. "Welcome to the Mixed-Up, Dialed-Down 2010 Whitney Biennial. *The Village Voice*, March 2, 2010.

Warner, Emily. "Theaster Gates." *Home Magazine*, May 10, 2009.

ATTA KIM

Atta Kim: ON-AIR. Germany: ICP/Steidl, 2006.

Atta Kim: The Museum Project. New York: Aperture Foundation, 2005.

Cotter, Holland. "When Real Time Turns Out to Be the Most Surreal of All." *The New York Times*, July 12, 2006.

Kim, Atta. "Boxing Kim." *Aperture,* Winter 2001.

Kim, Atta. *Water does not soak in rain*. Ostfildern: Hatje Cantz, 2009.

Pasulka, Nicole. "The Museum Project [Interview with Atta Kim]." *The Morning News*, August 7, 2006.

Sand, Olivia. "Atta Kim." *The Asian Art Newspaper*, November 2009.

WOLFGANG LAIB

4e Biennale de Lyon d'art contemporain. L'autre. Exhibition catalog, with text by Harald Szeemann. Lyon: Réunion des Musées Nationaux, 1997.

Jorgensen, Darren. "Wolfgang Laib: Returning to What Is. An Interview with Wolfgang Laib." *Melbourne Art Journal*, July–December 2005.

Kern, Hermann. *Wolfgang Laib*. München, Germany: Kunstraum München e.V, 1978.

Ottman, Klaus. "Wolfgang Laib." Interview. *Journal of Contemporary Art*, November 1986.

———. *Wolfgang Laib, A Retrospective*. Exhibition catalog, with essays by Margit Rowell, and a conversation between the artist and Harald Szeemann. American Federation of Arts and Hatje Cantz Publishers, 2000.

Page, Suzanne. "Wolfgang Laib," Interview. Barcelona: Fundació Joan Miró, 1989. Text by Margit Rowell.

Rowell, Margit. *Objects of Desire: the Modern Still Life*. Exhibition catalog. New York: The Museum of Modern Art, 1997.

Schwander, Martin. "Wolfgang Laib," Interview. De Pont Foundation, Tilburg, 1993. Text by Wilma van Asseldonk.

Singular Forms (Sometimes Repeated): Art from 1951 to the Present. Exhibition catalog. New York: Solomon R. Guggenheim Museum, 2004.

Weintraub, Linda. "Interview with Wolfgang Laib," *Art on the Edge and Over*, 1996, pp. 40–44.

The Whitechapel Art Gallery Centenary Review. Exhibition catalog. London: Whitechapel Art Gallery, 2001, p. 34.

Without Beginning Without End. April 17–July 16, 2007. Madrid: Museo Nacional Centro de Arte Reina Sofía, 2007.

Wolfgang Laib: Passageway-Overgoing, with essay by Seung-wan Kang. Korea: National Museum of Contemporary Art, 2003.

"Wolfgang Laib." Mönchengladbach, Germany: Katalog Biennale Venedig and Städtisches Museum Abteiberg, 1982–83. Text by Johannes Cladders.

CHARMION VON WIEGAND

Back to the Future: Alfred Jensen, Charmion von Wiegand, Simon Gouverneur, and the Cosmic Conversation. Exhibition catalog. Chicago: Loyola University, 2009.

Hersh, Jennifer Newton. *Abstraction, Spiritualism, and Social Justice: the Art and Writing of Charmion von Wiegand*. Thesis (Ph. D.). City University of New York, 1998.

Rowell, Margit. "Interview with Charmion von Wiegand." Solomon R. Guggenheim Museum (New York, N.Y.). *Piet Mondrian centennial exhibition*. New York: The Solomon R. Guggenheim Foundation, 1971.

Tworkov, Helen, and Stephen Westfall. *Charmion von Wiegand: An Artist's Path from Mondrian to Mantra January 1, 2007.* New York: Michael Rosenfeld Gallery, 2007.

von Wiegand, Charmion. *Charmion von Wiegand: Improvisations, 1945: September 9–November 1, 2003*. New York: Michael Rosenfeld Gallery. 2003.